The Race to the Top

The Race to the Top

THE REAL STORY OF GLOBALIZATION

Tomas Larsson

CATO
INSTITUTE
Washington, D.C.

Library of Congress Cataloging-in-Publication Data

Larsson, Tomas, 1966-
   [Världens klassresa. English]
   The race to the top : the real story of globalization / by Tomas Larsson.
      p. cm.
   "A revision and expansion of the book originally published by Timbro in
Swedish as Världens Klassresa (1999)"—Introd.
   Includes bibliographical references and index.
   ISBN 1-930865-14-7 (cloth)—ISBN 1-930865-15-5 (pbk)
   1. International trade—Social aspects. 2. International trade—Effect of
technological innovations on. 3. Free trade—Social aspects—Developing
countries. 4. Globalization—Economic aspects—Developing countries.
5. Globalization—Social aspects—Developing countries. 6. International
economic relations. I. Title.

HF1379 .L37 2001
337—dc21

                                                                    2001047315

Cover design by Elise Rivera.

Printed in the United States of America.

CATO INSTITUTE
1000 Massachusetts Ave., N.W.
Washington, D.C. 2001

Contents

Introduction

Mason Su is the founder of Iwill, a Taiwanese maker of computer boards. Iwill's products are much in demand among those with a need for speed. "Every day there is just one thought in my head," says Su. "Who's going to take my business away from me?" His customer base is global.

Seni Williams is a software manufacturer in a city without infrastructure, Lagos, in a country where the rules are always changing, Nigeria; he sells software nimble enough to tame the chaos. Flexibility is a virtue in the global market too—which is why not only Nigerians do business with him.

Prasit Visedpaitoon is the marketing manager of Thailand's Siam Cycle, which once upon a time exported 200,000 mountain bikes to countries throughout Europe. Until the day the European Commission in Brussels announced an "anti-dumping" investigation of bicycle exporters in Thailand, and the firm's export market dried up. Is Prasit a predator or a victim?

Zejna Kasic is a Bosnian refugee who knits pullovers for shivering Europeans. Her export trade was closed down by the foes of international competition. Predator or victim?

Kim Joo Young is a lawyer eager to help jump-start South Korean capitalism, a reform effort that has gotten a big boost in the wake of the Asian financial crises of 1997. His People's Solidarity for Participatory Democracy has already won a landmark case against the *chaebols*, mammoth government-propped corporations that flout the rules at the expense of stockholders. He wants South Korean markets to be shipshape by 2004.

These are the real people who, for good or ill, are caught in the thick of the accelerating world shrinkage that is globalization. Their tales are told in the pages that follow.

This story is not being reported from the bleachers. I, too, have been a player in the global market. A native of Sweden, I moved to Thailand in the autumn of 1990. I had studied Thai for three years at Lund University and was ready to put my knowledge to use. I

1

started by making the rounds of various newspapers and magazines in Bangkok, where I learned to write professionally in English (while polishing my Thai on the street). I soon realized that freelancing was more fun than being employed in one place.

It means variety. I have written for all sorts of newspapers and periodicals, from the editorial page of the Swedish financial daily *Finanstidningen*, where I publish a column, to the travel magazine *Vagabond*. From the *Financial Times* to the syndicalist *Arbetaren*. From *Sydsvenska Dagbladet* in my native Malmö to the *Far Eastern Economic Review* in Hong Kong.

Between 1992 and 1995 I was a correspondent for *Business Asia*, a Hong Kong-based newsletter published by the Economist Intelligence Unit. Editor Jamie Allen and I enjoyed an outstanding, fruitful partnership for three years, after which he resigned, turned freelance, and wrote a book about Hong Kong. I still don't know what the man looks like. We were in touch with each other just about every week during those three years. But we never met, nor have we since. Whenever I've been in Hong Kong, he's been off somewhere else. And whenever he's come to Bangkok, I've been off somewhere else. For three years, I had been drawn into the global economy without even knowing it was there.

That was just the beginning. I developed another productive long-distance relationship with a daily broadsheet in Stockholm, *Svenska Dagbladet*, for which I wrote columns and editorials from 1995 to 1999.

And I had an up-close-and-personal perspective on the multicultural society. Chanita, my wife, is Thai. But like nearly all Thais, she is something else too. In the United States they speak of hyphenated Americans. People are African-American, Chinese-American, Swedish-American. Chanita is Mon-Chinese-Thai. Our daughters are Mon-Chinese-Thai-Swedish. Martina, age six, and Carolina, age three, each speaks four languages: Thai, the family tongue; Mon, which their mother speaks with them; Swedish, which their father speaks with them; and English, which they learn in school and nursery. We are a global family.

When the Internet came to Thailand, I was curious to see whether the revolution could live up to its promises. Presumably, with the new technology you could live on a tropical island while working, on line, in snowbound Stockholm. That, at any rate, was the Swedish vision of things. The dream for someone who's been slogging away in Bangkok for seven years is to escape the increasing traffic jams and thickening fog of exhaust fumes. We moved to Phuket, an island in the south of Thailand which is sufficiently modernized (and globalized) to have a local Internet connection and a first-rate international airport. I am able to report that the new economy is as good as its word. You really can live on a tropical island while punching a clock in Stockholm, San Francisco, or Hong Kong. At all events, I can. (As you read this, I'm in Ithaca, New York, adding to my human capital. But that's another story.)

Like freelancers and project nomads everywhere, I rarely know where this month's rent is coming from. You come to deal with the uncertainty by working too much and worrying too much about the cash flow. Gradually, you learn to take things easier. Just when one project is running out, someone always sends an e-mail, asking if you would like to write something. And of course you would.

When P.J. Anders Linder, then managing director of Timbro, a Stockholm-based think tank, asked me if I would like to write a book about globalization, the answer was a foregone conclusion. This English-language edition is a revision and expansion of the book originally published by Timbro in Swedish as *Världens klassresa* (1999). My thanks to Roger Tanner for the translation and David M. Brown for editing assistance.

I don't claim to offer a comprehensive description or analysis of globalization, nor a panegyric of the onward global march of market forces. A good deal of that sort of thing has been published already.

Instead, this book provides a firsthand glimpse at what globalization means for people struggling to survive and prosper in economies all over the world. Although much of the story centers on Asia, I have sought to broaden the perspective and, accordingly, have included reportage, interviews, and ponderings inspired by trips to the United States, Brazil, and Germany.

Globalization is happening, faster and faster. But it is far from complete, and far from inevitable. Globalization can disrupt, but it can also empower. What does it all mean, for real people in the real workaday world? And where should we go from here? These are questions I've tried to answer.

1. Thailand—A Global Brothel

My journey to Pattaya—legendary Asian Sodom, notorious refuge of pedophiles and gangsters—had been inspired by a sleepless night at a "hotel" in the town of Trat, just a few hours to the south.

I'd missed the fact that the Trat Inn, which from the street looked just like any other hotel, was actually the town brothel. It didn't take long to get the picture, though. No one else seemed to be checking in with the intention of sleeping.

At about nine in the evening some 50 women and several transsexual men gathered in the corridor. As they awaited the arrival of their customers—who covered the spectrum from underage schoolboys to ancient fishermen—they smoked, smartened themselves up, and fortified themselves with strong drink.

There I met 21-year-old Kai (her name means "chicken"), who seemed permanently on the point of tears. Her eyes darted hither and thither and her fingers eternally fidgeted. She had a bruise on her left cheek. She was from the neighboring town of Chantaburi, known for its rubies, and had grown up in a broken family. There were 10 other children, with a sequence of different mothers and fathers. Kai had a son of her own, she said, whom she had left in an orphanage after the father, a soldier, refused to have anything to do with either of them.

She'd been in the game since her teens, selling her body in hopes of saving money and getting rich. So far it wasn't working very well. Kai was in debt to the proprietor of the brothel after borrowing money for a cassette player. She dreamed of selling herself to wealthy foreign tourists instead of to the local Thai yokels. Pattaya was where the dreams would be realized.

"If only I can pay off the debt on the cassette player, I'll go to Pattaya," she told me.

My night at the Trat Inn was a troubled one. First the power failed. One of the women panicked and began running to and fro and screaming "Klua phi! Klua phi!" ("I'm afraid of the ghost! I'm afraid of the ghost!"). Then candles were found and calm was restored until the customers began arriving in drunken contingents. One by one, the doors of the small rooms slammed shut. Later, running water could be heard through the thin walls as the ladies showered between tricks.

When I left my room early in the morning, a beautiful young woman and an elderly man stood waiting in the corridor; all the other rooms were occupied, apparently. As soon as I emerged they threw themselves onto the bed, which was still warm from my body. The night's final demonstration of virility was about to take place. I caught the bus to Pattaya.

At the time of my visit to the Trat Inn, the term "globalization" had not yet penetrated the Thai language, but it would be fair to say that Kai wanted to globalize herself. Pattaya represented a step up for her. She realized, of course, that the nature of the work wouldn't change. But the pay was better in the globalized bars of Pattaya than in the isolated Trat Inn. Conditions would be better. Pattaya, as Kai saw it, was the better of two bad situations.

But there was more to Pattaya than its seedy globalized under-belly. There was plenty of healthy bourgeois ordinariness, too. On the beach, gray-haired British ladies sat in a long line reading airport paperbacks. Elderly couples walked hand-in-hand along the prome-nade, the women in floral-patterned summer dresses and the men in short-sleeved shirts, khaki Bermuda shorts, and knee-length white socks. It seemed more like a European health resort than a den of iniquity.

European tourists were getting away from it all thanks to newly globalized package tours. Mediterranean resorts had become com-monplace, so the travel industry had begun organizing tours to exotic parts of Asia—including Pattaya—that until then had de-terred everyone but Joseph Conrad, Somerset Maugham, war corre-spondents, and sundry other adventurers.

Not that Pattaya was Europeanized through and through. The ho-tel discos were crowded with trendy Thai yuppies, who also streamed into the town's excellent seafood restaurants to wolf down shrimp, crab, and fish. Thai families on weekend excursions from Bangkok were everywhere, the youngsters splashing at the water's edge on Jomtien beach and in the hotel pools while their mothers and fathers relaxed under parasols munching papaya salads or sipping whisky and water. Mobile phones were lined up on the small beach tables. New cars bearing Bangkok registration plates filled the hotel parking spaces.

The notorious bathing resort where youngish westerners are said to occupy their days with surfeits of sun, sex, and drugs had now been invaded by a newly enriched middle class. To be sure, these Bangkok citizens did not lack a touch of the European in the trademarks they sported: Johnnie Walker and Chivas Regal, Ericsson and Nokia, Mercedes-Benz and Volvo. The well-heeled Thai middle class were the new kings of Pattaya. And they were as global as any foreign tourist.

They were the product of Thailand's strong export industry and massive foreign investments, which, starting in the mid-1980s, had in the space of a few years transformed Thailand from a sluggish backwater in the shadow of the Vietnam War to an incandescent, industrialized "miracle."

The traditional Northern European sex tourists did not abandon Pattaya altogether. One or two specimens could still be seen on rented motor bikes with their rented Thai girlfriends perched on the pillions. But in the broad light of day, at least, they disappeared among the gray panthers and Thai yuppies. To find the old Pattaya, you had to scout the back streets.

Walking through town, I came upon a restaurant named MacSweden. I dropped in for a cup of coffee. MacSweden was as deserted as the depopulated rural regions of Sweden itself. The plastic restaurant tables were empty. Fading posters of Björn Borg, Ingemar Stenmark, and the good old national idols hung from the walls. Peace and quiet reigned, a rarity in noisy, hectic Thailand.

MacSweden represented the good old days. Good old Sweden. Good old honest Swedishness. Now available in Thailand.

MacSweden welcomed its guests with signs proclaiming native Swedish dishes and "No Arabs."

* * *

It's easy to moralize about human exploitation in Thailand, Pattaya in particular. Even as we deplore it, though, we should remember that the alternatives—like the Trat Inn—are often nastier still. Sex tourism in Pattaya tells us less about Pattaya than about the economic and cultural dysfunction of Trat, Chantaburi, and other places in Thailand. Pattaya is the symptom. The disease itself is located in the towns and villages exporting their sons and daughters to Pattaya—and in the capital, Bangkok, where all the political decisions are made.

Foreign exploitation of Thai resources assumes perhaps its most brutal manifestation in the sex industry. But to Kai and her colleagues—just as for the child workers of the small workshops—school and ordinary employment are not genuine options. They make their way to the Trat Inn, Pattaya, and illegal factories for lack of better alternatives. They do not end up there solely because of the demand for commercial sex and the labor of deft little fingers.

Whence the lack of alternatives, then? Where does the fault lie? Partly, it springs from a lack of education, examples, and imagination. Perhaps Kai cannot imagine the alternatives, even if they do exist.

Some would insist that the fault lies with the human habit of exploitation, and particularly with its great modern enabler, economic globalization—what some critics call "Brazilianization." The rich get richer and the poor and downtrodden just get more poor and more downtrodden.

Is that what globalization is all about?

And what's Brazil got to do with it?

2. Brazilianization

Brazil enjoys a special position in the debate over globalization. It is often described as global capitalism in microcosm, a harbinger of things to come.

If the forces of economic globalization are allowed free play, we're told, then the United States and Europe—indeed, the whole world—will soon end up looking just like Brazil, the country often thought to suffer the globe's most glaring income gaps. Globalization is then Brazilianization.

But what is globalization?

Simply put, it is the process of world shrinkage, of distances getting shorter, things moving closer. It pertains to the increasing ease with which somebody on one side of the world can interact, to mutual benefit, with somebody on the other side of the world.

Of course, globalization as such is nothing new, dating at least from the first world-circling trade routes that emerged out of the embers of the Middle Ages. In the very busy century just ended, though, the pace zoomed. Every big advance affecting transportation or communication—the telephone, airplane, TV, and computer, and now the Internet, wireless phones, and wireless e-mail—has served to bring us closer together.

In the 1990s, globalization was the "next big thing." From Bangkok to Stockholm and from Paris to Santiago, the theme kept cropping up. The dangers. The possibilities. Individuals and nations have been fretting over it, struggling to cope with it, or hoping the next big wave of it will lift them to an easier and richer future.

The most recent wave of globalization was impelled by two historic events: the economic advance of Asia since the 1960s, and the collapse of Soviet communism in Europe, starting in 1989. Both Asia and Eastern Europe quickly migrated toward western society, economically especially, but also politically and culturally. Trade and investment, democratization, rock stars, and Hollywood blockbusters were the manifestations.

Technology also played a role. The Internet and other electronic networks make it possible for more and more people all over the world to conquer physical distances. If you're on one side of the planet and I'm on the other, it's easier than ever these days for us to be trading partners—and friends. Transactions that once took months, weeks, days, are now taking hours, minutes, seconds. When I moved to Bangkok in 1990, catching up on the news back home meant scavenging the Scandinavian restaurants for the Swedish newspapers donated by kindhearted tourists or SAS pilots. With luck, the newspapers might be current. Today I can read the day's Swedish news with my early morning coffee. It takes just a few seconds to call up *Svenska Dagbladet*'s virtual front page on my computer screen, at the cost of a local phone call.

But I believe that history and politics have been more pivotal than the information revolution. Globalization is a hot topic largely thanks to the dramatic growth of Asian trade and industry over the past few decades. Sixty percent of the world's population lives in Asia. Economic liberalization in China and India have put more than two billion people in touch with global markets and cultures. Between 1985 and 1997, East and Southeast Asia almost doubled their share of the total value of foreign direct investments in the world economy. Thirty of the world's 50 biggest transnational corporations based outside the traditional industrialized nations are headquartered in Asian economies like South Korea, China, Hong Kong, Taiwan, Singapore, and Malaysia. Without the Asian economic "miracle"—and its ripple effect on Latin America and Africa—there would not be so many Internet servers and personal computers in what was once known as the Third World. The collapse of communism in what was once known as the Second World added still more to the mix. Without Asia and Eastern Europe, globalization would have remained the internal concern of the wealthiest industrialized nations—the United States, the European Union, and Japan. Instead, slowly but surely, globalization is becoming. . .well, global.

Thailand's economy is small in relation to the Asian giants, but its growth has been all the faster. Between the mid-1980s and mid-1990s, Thailand was the world's fastest-growing economy, with an average annual GNP per capita growth rate of 8.4 percent. In Thailand as in the rest of the region, the economic upturn means ordinary people are able to lead better lives, with better food, better education, better health care. Within the space of one generation, millions of Thais—and hundreds of millions of other Asians—have left poverty and misery behind them and have joined the global middle class.

Horrible, this Brazilianization!

* * *

So far as I know, the link between Brazil and the effects of globalization was first explored by the German journalists Hans-Peter Martin and Harald Schumann in their widely noticed 1996 book, *The Global Trap*. Martin and Schumann describe the affluent residential area of Alphaville, outside São Paulo, where prosperous members of the middle class surround themselves with several-meter-high walls armed with searchlights and electronic detectors sensitive to the slightest movement. Security is also guaranteed by stringent surveillance routines.

On the prowl for intruders, private security guards (who often have a second job with the military police) cruise day and night around Alphaville on motorcycles and in military vehicles with military signaling lights. Workmen, tradesmen, and other unknown people must show ID before gaining entry to this rich man's ghetto; they're body-searched on their way out, just in case they've stolen anything. If any unauthorized person slips through the security and is detected within the perimeter, the guards, armed with revolvers and sawn-off shotguns, don't hesitate to shoot first and ask questions later.

Alphaville, the authors find, is an ideal refuge for those residents of the metropolis who fear downtown criminals and subversives, want to live like ordinary families in Europe or the United States, and can get along just fine without direct exposure to the social reality of their own country.

Martin and Schumann convey a frightening picture of Brazil. They also maintain that, as a result of globalization, Brazil is becoming a "world model." The economic and political élites of the affluent western world are as deceitful as those of Brazil, they say; and the European upper classes, too, are beginning to take refuge behind Alphaville-like enclaves. If we want to know what's in store for the countries walking into the global trap, all we have to do is take a look at São Paulo and Rio de Janeiro.

Thomas L. Friedman, foreign affairs columnist on the *New York Times*, is on the same track. In his book *The Lexus and the Olive Tree*, published in 1999, he argues that globalization is in process of creating a "winner-take-all" world—a world in which the winners grab the whole of the market, leaving the rest of us to squabble over the crumbs. "The more that different markets get globalized and become winners-take-all markets, the more inequality expands within countries and, for that matter, between countries," he argues. He regards this un-egalitarian propensity as "globalization's Achilles' heel." This Achilles' heel is exemplified in part by the enormous economic gaps in Rio de Janeiro, and in part by the economic crisis of 1998, which forced the Brazilian government to slash spending.

The picture popular journalists have painted of the relationship between the Brazilian model and globalization has been the linchpin of more intellectually sophisticated analysis too. The German sociologist Ulrich Beck, professor at the University of Munich and at the London School of Economics, warns us against the "Brazilianization of Europe" that will ensue if globalization is allowed to continue. Here is Beck's description of a Brazilianized Europe, which will emerge in an era when nation-states have withered away and "the United Nations has been superseded by an association styling itself United Coca-Cola":

> The neo-liberals have been victorious. Over themselves as well. The national state has been swept away. The welfare state lies in ruins. But a non-order prevails. The edifice of power and law belonging to the players of the national state has been superseded by innumerable more or less obscure power organizations doing battle with each other. Between them lies a legal and normative no-man's land. . . .
>
> Armed troops of pensioners patrol the frontier of their affluent senior housing units. . . .
>
> Anyone venturing into the still-open subway stations is asking to be mugged. Having been mugged amounts to a self-indictment, the rule being that those who are attacked have only themselves to blame. . . .
>
> Payment of tax has for a long time, de facto at least, been eleemosynary, and taxes are paid in competition with other tributes and levies for protection which the powerful security organizations collect with their saber-rattling, the national monopoly of force having long since been abolished together with all other monopolies.

Beck maintains that without a strong European defense against the ravaging forces of globalization, European high civilization will devolve into a Brazilian dystopia. Globalization means collapse, pure and simple.

Another professor at the London School of Economics, philosopher John Gray, sings a similar tune. As early as 1990—several years before *The Global Trap* saw print—Gray described what he called "the Brazilianization of the United States." At that time the term "globalization" had yet to gain widespread currency. But Gray would return to the theme in his 1999 book, *False Dawn*. The threat of globalization, he therein claims, consists not so much in an American Balkanization, a process in which societies are splintered on racial grounds, as in a Brazilianization, which divides races into separate and unequal classes, with blacks as the lower class and whites as the upper class. The premier proof of the ongoing Brazilianization of the United States is America's wanton incarceration of such a large proportion of its young black men.

Per Gray, this sort of Brazilianization is a uniquely American phenomenon, something that does not exist and cannot happen in Europe. "The confluence of ethnic and economic divisions and antagonisms in the United States is not found in any other First World country. The free market has produced a mutation in American capitalism, as a consequence of which it is coming to resemble the oligarchical regimes of some Latin American countries more than the liberal capitalist civilization of Europe, or of the United States itself in earlier phases of its history."

Unlike Beck, Gray does not foresee a Brazilianized Europe. Otherwise, though, their visions are similar: Both argue that globalization is tearing away at the European "model" of social democracy and welfare state. In any case, says Gray, the runaway laissez-faire capitalism now dominating the globe will soon collapse under the weight of speculative excesses and social retrogression. We should start sketching a new European alternative right away, so it'll be ready to put in place as soon as the collapse happens.

A Brazilian motif also informs Polish sociologist Zygmunt Bauman's analysis of globalization. In his book *Globalization: The Human Consequences*, Bauman propounds the thesis that globalization is spawning a new social stratification in which wealth and liberty are global, while poverty and constraint are local. Bauman maintains that globalization will transform the traditional nation-state into a nightwatchman state whose main and only task in the new era will be one of policing. The state will be obliged to create the law and order demanded by nomadic global capital and the élite that shuffles it.

The "Brazilian" view of globalization, although not invariably formulated in such terms, quickly made its way into the debating lists. In his widely noted book *The Work of Nations*, Robert B. Reich, once President Clinton's labor secretary, claimed that the economic élites are in the process of betraying their national communities. According to Reich, the so-called symbolic analysts—the highly paid intellectual workers of the new IT economy—have become social separatists. They neither feel nor assume any responsibility for their fellow beings, and certainly have no intention of financing the welfare state. The rules of the game in the new economy spell the end of a common national destiny. Reich agrees that the prosperous élites are isolating themselves in their enclaves and abandoning an increasingly impoverished population to its terrible fate.

"All Americans used to be in roughly the same economic boat," Reich tells us. "Most rose or fell together, as the corporations in which they were employed, the industries comprising such corporations, and the national economy as a whole became more productive—or languished. But national boundaries no longer define our economic fates. We are now in different boats, one sinking rapidly, one sinking more slowly, and the third rising steadily." Globalization means that the more fortunate fifth of the American labor force no longer feels any community of destiny with the less fortunate four-fifths. On these newly segregated economic boats, social solidarity is ballast to be cast overboard.

The process of Brazilianization may be summed up as follows. The rich are getting richer and fewer, the poor are getting poorer and more numerous. The growing economic polarization leads to a geographical separation, an apartheid between the local and the global that is enforced by creating special enclaves for the rich and stashing the poor in prison. Thus, the self-imposed isolation of the western middle class in special residential areas, and the other-imposed isolation of the underclass filling prisons to the bursting point, are two sides of the same "Brazilian" coin.

In globalization, Brazilian-style, a small, exclusive group travels by express elevator to the economic top, while the rest, *lumpenproletariat* or permanently unemployed, plunge to the dungeons.

Clearly, then, Brazil must be a terribly unpleasant place.

3. The Real 20/80 Society

The traffic has ground to a halt. Outside the American School, educator of the children of the elite, a man lies inert, his feet propped against the curb, his head in the middle of the carriageway. The man's face has been beaten to a pulp and a dark pool is spreading beneath his back. Police stand guard in a circle, looking official. Boys rush down from the slums to gape. By the time the resulting traffic jam has been sorted out, the blood is slowly seeping down the hill.

The slums of Rio can be dreadfully violent, especially when wars erupt between rival drug syndicates or between syndicates and the police. Though Rocinha is only a few minutes' drive from the high-class districts of Leblon and Ipanema, it is wild, lawless territory. Brazilian police armed with automatic weapons move through the slums in teams, preferring to keep to the main streets. They operate like an occupying power. And they don't have many friends among the locals.

The real source of law and order in Rocinha is "the Red Commando," a criminal syndicate with communist roots that nowadays keeps busy with drug trafficking. My guide explains that in practice, it's safer to live up in the slums than down in the city. Bloody turf wars there may be, but the Mafia will not condone theft and other crimes on its own territory. So the doors in the slums are unlocked, while down in Rio the residents live behind bars and locks. By Rio standards, the two banks in Rocinha are unique: They've never known an armed robbery. Luiz Soares, a Workers Party member who handled public security in Rio de Janeiro for more than a year, told attendees of a recent World Social Forum at Porto Alegre that "the people [in the shantytowns] fear the police more than the drug dealers because the latter, though they torture and extort, are at least predictable. . .while the police are as violent, but unpredictable."

Rocinha is governed by organized crime. And Rio is governed by politicians who recently awarded honorary citizenship to a representative of another kind of organized crime—Fidel Castro, the

15

leader of Cuban Stalinism. No wonder bloody fighting erupts from time to time between the rival robber bands of Brazilian society.

* * *

Rio is the world turned upside down. The poor live in first-class locations, on the mountainsides, enjoying what may be the loveliest view in the world—high above the city, the beaches, the sea. Meantime, the wealthy huddle in the center of town with little to gaze upon but congested streets and the facades of buildings across the way. Not that the slums are idyllic. Walking between the buildings, many of which are three or four stories high, through a maze of narrow lanes, can be claustrophobic—like being trapped in a human anthill. But then there's that mountain air and panoramic view.

In Rio, multimillionaires live side by side with slum-dwellers who must get by on less than a dollar a day. According to statistical tables published by the World Bank, only Sierra Leone, with its population of five million, has a more unequal distribution of incomes than this largest country in Latin America, population 161 million.

True, tables of this kind are to be taken with a grain of salt. Many countries do not report any comparable figures at all. And in countries like Brazil, with a large informal sector, economic statistics are indeed of dubious reliability. But no one seriously disputes the fact that Brazil has enormous disparities in living standards between the rich minority and the poor majority, and that those differences are greater than in most other countries.

Such disparities are far from the whole story, however. Rio de Janeiro has been described as a bit of Paris surrounded by a chunk of Ethiopia. But without romanticizing poverty and gangster rule, it's clear that life in a well-established slum like Rocinha is not quite as bad as all that. In the past few years the slum has been refrigerated, telephonized, globalized.

It is in Rocinha—not the sleepy business districts of Rio, frequented by the élites—that Brazil's progress in recent years is most visible. The *favelas*, shantytowns, are dynamic, hopping. Viewed from above, Rocinha is a forest of small-dish aerials. In the small shops lining the main street you can buy refrigerators from Asia and mobile phones from Finland. You can pay for your new shoes with Mastercard or Visa. Dentists and lawyers have opened up practices on new premises. Through the open windows of shantytown dwellings, what you see is not necessarily appalling poverty; you're just as likely to spot a neat living room complete with television, VCR, and computer. In 1999, the *New York Times* reported that Rocinha had more than 2,000 shops and companies, five banks and credit institutions, three daily newspapers, even its own home page on the Internet (http://rocinha.com.br). Plus a McDonald's has set up shop. When the golden arches come to town, you know you're going global.

"Class differences in Brazil have been reduced by globalization," says Lennart Palmeus, Latin American correspondent for the Swedish business daily *Dagens Industri*. Lennart has been living in Rio since the early 1980s. "I know people who were literally starving 10 years ago, who now have both fridges and computers."

During Fernando Henrique Cardoso's time as finance minister and then president, Brazil has broken with chronic hyper-inflation and opened its market to foreign competition. These economic reforms have struck hard at those who benefited from protectionism, and who resent the loss of privilege, but they have brought growing prosperity for the poorest Brazilians.

Norberto Albrecht is a taxi driver in Rio. His grandparents came to Brazil from Germany in 1922. He has two daughters, aged 10 and 14. Albrecht hates his new job. For 20 years he worked as a quality controller in a plastics factory. Two years ago he was put out of work.

"The politicians opened up the borders to imports and we were put out of business by the South Koreans," he recalls morosely. "Brazil was a better place 10 or 20 years ago. I didn't like the military dictatorship, but life was better. My quality of life has deteriorated. In those days I worked an eight-hour day. Now I have to work 15 hours a day for the same amount of money."

Albrecht blames the decline in his fortunes on the politicians. "Politics," he sighs. "Someone ought to bomb the Congress. Then we could start all over again."

"We of the middle class are having a difficult time at present," says Fernando de Albuquerque, a business consultant who studied at Stanford. "My money goes to the poor. Ten years ago I had twice the purchasing power I have now. The poor are taking money away from the middle class. Their purchasing power has improved, but the economy hasn't grown."

Ten years ago, before the economy was opened up, life in Brazil was doubtless better for Albrecht and Albuquerque than it is today.

But for the inhabitants of Rocinha and Rio's 600 other *favelas*, things have improved dramatically—economically, socially, medically. Globalization in Brazil is indeed resulting in a 20/80 society, but not as normally understood: the prosperous 20 per cent are now worse off, while the poorest 80 per cent are better off.

During the 1990s, nearly 20 million Brazilians entered the lower middle class. Many of them have been able to buy mobile phones and PCs as well as TV sets and fridges. And, of course, they have been able to fill those fridges with food and drink. Compare that to the 1980s, when one in five Brazilians went hungry every day. So perhaps it is not so tragic if members of the steel industry—and other skilled workers—find they must struggle to adapt to the new, more competitive, more global economy.

Ignoring for the moment the direction the economic winds have been blowing, we can acknowledge the brute fact that tens of millions of Brazilians still live in what is technically termed "absolute poverty" (with incomes of less than a dollar a day), even as the élite idle on the sun-baked beaches of Ipanema and Copacabana. But does this economic reality portend what is in store for the rest of the world, should the forces of globalization be allowed unfettered sway? One necessary premise of the now familiar argument is that Brazil's misfortune and injustice—like Thailand's misfortune and injustice—are the products of the very globalization and economic liberalization against which Beck and the rest are warning us.

But maybe we need to look elsewhere for the causes of Thailand's "Brazilianization"—and even Brazil's.

4. Legacies of the Ipanema Left

The paradox, of course, is that despite all the hand-wringing about Brazilian globalization and the race to the bottom, the history of Brazilianized Brazil has hardly been distinguished by unfettered markets and untrammeled trade. Historian Marshall Eakin observes that while the nationalists who fashioned modern Brazil may have sung the gospel of liberal capitalism, they crafted the most state-controlled economy outside the communist bloc. Liberalization has been belated, uneven, and recent. The critics are wearing blinders.

In Brazil, as in most other Latin American countries, the consensus in favor of the closed economy was broad. And the sentiment persists. Harvard economist Jeffrey Sachs considers Brazil to be "chronically introverted." As recently as 1998, the country's total exports made up just six percent of its entire output, placing Brazil in the same rank as countries like Haiti and Rwanda (hardly showcases of globalization). No other major economy has such a low figure. Ironically, the Brazilian left is now campaigning for a continuation of the economic policy of the right-wing generals: state ownership rather than private ownership, protectionism rather than free trade, intervention rather than the free play of the market.

Not until he found himself building roads in Nyerere's Tanzania, in 1980, did the late Brazilian entrepreneur Donald Stewart Jr. realize that Brazil was then a socialist country too. That would seem to be a hard fact to miss, but the military, which formulated economic policy, ardently professed to be combating anything to do with communism and socialism.

In Brazil the ideology prompting the state's dominant role in the economy was nationalist rather than socialist. The leaders aimed to create a great economic and political power. Jucelino Kubitschek, president between 1956 and 1961, declared Brazil would develop "fifty years in five." And, in a manner of speaking, the Brazilians have accomplished that. In 1950 or so theirs was the fiftieth largest economy in the world. By the 1970s it had become the world's tenth largest. From the 1870s to the 1980s, Brazilian per capita income rose by 1,100 percent, a pace surpassed only by Japan. Unlike the Japanese, though, millions of Brazilians are still living in abject poverty.

The Brazilian example shows that "economic growth" as such is by no means a cure-all. It has to be enjoyed more or less across the board. And it can be, if there's no artificial steering of wealth to one group at the expense of another. Instead, incomes in Brazil became extremely polarized, thanks to the country's industrialization strategy of protecting industry by high tariff walls and expansionist financial policies that bankrolled numerous so-called strategic projects and industries. Brazil scraped along by feverish borrowing and spending. The holes in the national budget were plugged mostly with international loans and flurries of funny money. Brazil learned to live with high inflation for decade after decade. As recently as 1993, the annual inflation rate was a whopping 2,500 per cent—a national record.

The result was a torrential transfer of real wealth from the poorest to the richest. The rich were able to guard against inflation by investing money abroad or in Brazilian banks, where interest rates were index-adjusted. But the poor did not even have bank books. So the nation's frantic destruction of capital meant the frantic destruction of *their* capital.

"In Rio we sometimes had 3 percent inflation per day," recalled Stewart. "For the poorest, this meant that the money they earned one day lost 30 per cent of its value within ten days."

No wonder so few Brazilians were able to save up for a refrigerator.

"The higher classes can protect themselves, even profit from inflation. The poor have no escape, they just get poorer and poorer," said Stewart, who, after his visit to Tanzania, founded Brazil's first liberal think-tank.

Lenin argued that there is no more subtle and sure way to wreck the foundations of a society than to destroy its currency. In just the years since 1986, Brazil has churned through six different currencies! But the systematic destruction of these monies has merely reinforced the status quo. That revolution never came to Brazil probably had a lot to do with the social safety valves provided by the carnival, the samba, and football. It probably also had something to do with the fact that the socialists in Brazil were and are on the "wrong" side— the side of the undeservedly prosperous elite—of the so-called class struggle.

Antonio Carlos Pôrto Gonçalves, head of the Instituto Brasileiro de Economia (IBRE), an economic research institute, explains: "The left in Brazil is a left that doesn't care about the poor. It cares about national government employees, about the company employees who will lose their jobs when protectionism disappears, and about 50-year-olds drawing pensions of 20,000 dollars a month."

If globalization does indeed spell the collapse of the welfare state (a big if), that would not necessarily be unwelcome. It could even mean greater social justice. Especially for countries like Brazil, where the state subsidizes the homes of the tiny middle class, but not those of the large lower class. And where the education budget is spent on fine universities for the well-off, but not on compulsory schools for the poor.

"Ninety percent of Brazil's social budget goes to the wealthiest 10 percent of the population," says *Dagens Industri* correspondent Lennart Palmeus.

Powerful vested interests are favored. The military, for example, annually contributes some 100 million reals to the social security system, but gets back 7.2 billion. The biggest and politically most influential interest group, though, is the pensioners. Federal civil servants pay 3.3 billion reals into the pension system each year, but pull out nearly 13 billion. Things are not much better in the individual states. On average, a third of their current budgets go to pensions. National government employees receive pensions that average eight times higher than those received by private sector employees. So, when the welfare state finds itself in crisis and must try to slim down, it's not the residents of the Rocinha shantytowns who protest, but the reactionary upper class of nearby Ipanema.

Fortunately, the Ipanema left—a term I borrow from Palmeus—failed to halt the economic reforms that were inaugurated during the 1990s with notably good results. Inflation was curbed. Words like privatization and competition entered the political vocabulary, and even pension reform is now on the agenda (though it's far from certain it can overcome political obstacles). In the space of 10 years, the cost of a mobile phone dropped from $38,000 to less than $200. It no longer took a decade to get a permanent telephone line. And it suddenly became legal again to buy imported information technology. In the 1980s Brazil had perversely banned all IT imports, an industrial Kim-Il-Sung-ism that was supposed to transform Brazil into a great IT power. All it really did, of course, was enable far too many sheltered Brazilian companies to make far too hefty a profit for far too many years with utterly substandard technology.

Privatization has not yet been attended by reform of the government's spending habits, though; instead, the benefits of the former have tended to mask the consequences of the latter. During the 1990s, the state's deficit only grew (as did foreign-born debt to finance it). Selling state assets generated lots of revenue, but there are limits to how much a government can auction off. In the wake of the Russian default in 1998, doubts began to emerge in financial markets about the sustainability of the Brazilian trend, and the worries helped send the real plummeting again. But one habit *had* changed: the printing press was no longer the solution of first resort in monetary crises. In September 1998, when the new round of troubles started for Brazil, the inflation rate was under 3 percent a year. But even after the real suffered a 30 percent drop in value in the new exchange-rate regime, inflation remained surprisingly low, around 4 percent a year. That's restraint.

Nonetheless, the latest disturbance has been blamed on "money markets" and globalization, as if the rampant money-printing of the pre-reform era, and its bloated budgets, had never blighted the exchequer. Net-net, Brazil is better off in the wake of globalization and economic reforms. And it makes sense that a recovering economy, like any convalescent, will suffer the aftereffects of its past illness, especially if the cure is not yet complete. Getting sick again is hardly the solution.

The danger to Brazil—and to many other countries in the same boat—lies not in speculation by foreign hedge funds or any other capitalist villainy, but in the persistent excesses of its politicians. Despite improvements elsewhere, Brazil's national bureaucracy is still growing without restraint. The expenditures associated with the nation's absurd pension system still exceed all reasonable bounds. The Brazilian state is still taking from the poor and giving to the rich. And so the poor are responding by organizing themselves into slum societies the state cannot reach, willing to be governed by the Red Commando and other gangs, but not by elected officials.

The systematic civil disobedience and Mafia rule in Rocinha are indeed a reaction, but not against runaway global capitalism. They are a response to the tragic perversions of a still largely incorrigible rentier state.

5. The Isolation Trap

And "Brazilianized" Thailand? Again, economy-thumping government policies have been more responsible for the plight of the residents of the Trat Inn than has the bogeyman of globalization.

On the way from Trat to Pattaya you pass through the town of Rayong, bulging with petrochemical plants and car factories. These might be taken as proof of Thailand's successful industrialization strategy, but in fact they are evidence of political perversity. The country's rulers have been more concerned with building up prestigious heavy industry than with making proper jobs possible for Kai and other young people. By means of minimum wages, tax breaks for heavy industry, protectionist trade policy, and other interventions, Bangkok has lured certain industries to invest in Thailand, scared others away. The result: Thailand's industrial structure is off-kilter—skewed both geographically and economically.

Geographically, Thailand's industry is clustered around Bangkok and Rayong. The rest of the country has practically nothing. Greater Bangkok in 1990 accounted for 76 percent of the country's total industrial output and 55 percent of Thailand's gross domestic product.

It has been remarked that Bangkok *is* Thailand. Administratively, there's no doubt about it. I experienced the bureaucratic reality first-hand when I sought passports for my newborn, Carolina. Having both Swedish and Thai citizenship, she needed two. The Swedish passport was a piece of cake. We had merely to visit the Swedish consulate in Phuket in the south of Thailand, where we were living at the time, and submit our application. Then there was the Thai passport. To apply for that one we had to journey more than 500 miles to the capital. Apparently it doesn't occur to the Thai bureaucracy that somebody outside Bangkok might like a passport. Extreme administrative centralization of this kind is not the exception but the rule. Far too many permits and licenses are issued in Bangkok and nowhere else.

Bangkok *is* Thailand economically, as well. This is no coincidence. Obviously, companies will be reluctant to set up shop in the countryside when all dealings with the authorities must take place in the capital. But the deck is also stacked in other ways. While local manufacturing is heavily subsidized, rural development is ignored, even penalized, with punitive taxes levied on rice exports. In consequence, industry is far too capital-intensive in relation to the country's level of development. And of course, the propped-up manufacturing sector has a relatively greater need for engineers and business administration graduates than for unskilled people like Kai, for whom the most plausible avenues of advancement are fore-closed. It is thus not the market, but the state's interference with the market, that breeds the social and economic injustices so blatant in Pattaya.

Here we are confronted with a dreary irony. Countries like Thailand are often charged with practicing "social dumping," which they accomplish by banking on low-paid industry. "Unfair competition!" bleat the union leaders of affluent western countries. But the real problem is typically the opposite. Far from pushing an inhuman low-pay strategy, Thailand has rolled all its policy dice on the high-paid industries. The statutory minimum wage has been pitched so high that hiring the least-skilled and therefore least-productive workers has become uneconomical. There is no place for them in the car factories or the petrochemical plants. There is no place for them in the export-oriented electronics factories that are jam-packed with sophisticated machinery, either. True, these industries have created jobs for millions of Thai workers, which in its way is an impressive success. But at the same time, Kai and millions of others have been excluded from the labor market—even as the government's industrial policy jacks up the cost of living.

But they've got to make a living all the same. Many do so by staying on in the countryside: More than half the Thai population have agriculture as their main source of income. But many are turning in mounting desperation to the Trat Inn, Pattaya, the illegal sweatshops. Such informal, illegal, and mostly health-endangering sectors of the Thai economy have, regrettably, become the only real option for these people.

It is often alleged that free trade, free flow of capital, and rapid economic growth widen the income gaps in society. The claim just doesn't tally with the facts. By all standard yardsticks of economic inequality, Thailand is the country in East and Southeast Asia with the biggest economic gaps. It is also the country where inequality has been growing fastest in recent decades. But the growing injustices of the Thai economy have little to do with any brutal global market forces. The racist "No Arabs" sign adorning the MacSweden of Pattaya has its counterpart in the economic policy of protectionism. All manner of taxes and regulations fend off foreign goods and foreign capital. During the 1990s, Thailand's customs tariffs were among the highest in the world: The average in 1993 was more than 45 percent, sky-high compared with the 5 to 15 percent that are termed normal. Sort of makes it harder for cheaper goods to get into the country.

It wasn't always this way. As the 1960s opened, Thailand boasted the lowest import tariffs in Asia. But then the tariff walls were quickly flung up to levels far greater than those of the other tigers. When tariffs increase, so do domestic costs; in the absence of foreign competition, protected companies can raise their prices more than they would have otherwise. They can also afford to pay their workers more than their production would be worth on the open market. And while labor costs are artificially raised in certain parts of the economy (the protected parts), they must become correspondingly depressed in other parts (the non-protected ones). This is what happened. It certainly became harder to make a living in the agricultural sector. Export quotas for leading agricultural products like rubber, tapioca, and rice didn't help matters either. In 1980, rice was the single largest export product. It has since been replaced by garments, computer parts, jewelry, plastics, prawns, rubber, integrated circuits, and industrial products. High export tariffs on rice hit hard at the incomes of those living in the countryside. That's economic injustice— the injustice of an *anti*-globalization policy.

There is a Brazilianesque logic to Thailand's protectionism: It takes from the poor and gives to the rich. It has been the Thai farmers—60 percent of the labor force in 1994—who have had to subsidize the protectionist industrial policy benefiting Bangkok. This absurd development strategy is reflected in the income tables for the different Thai provinces. The list is topped by Bangkok and vicinity, with an average income of 186,167 baht ($7,118) in 1994, more than triple the national average of 61,335 baht per capita. At the bottom of the barrel is Sisaket, a province in northeastern Thailand, where the average income that year was 14,960 baht (about $572). It took 12 people in Sisaket to produce as much wealth as one person in Bangkok.

Depressing the farmers' incomes by political means was of course not a sound recipe for economic success. The worst effect has been that poor Thai families cannot afford to properly educate their children. The problem is not, as one might suspect, that they are forced to send the children to work instead of school to help provide for the family; they have enough to survive, at any rate. The real problem, according to an analysis by the World Bank, is that rural families have not been earning enough money to pay for their children's schooling expenses—school uniforms, books, and all the rest of it. The schools were there, as were the teachers. But families like Kai's cannot afford to send their youngsters to school for much more than the four (now six) years that are compulsory.

Does this description of the Thai economy clash with the conventional image of Thailand as a low-wage country with a rapidly expanding export industry? Not necessarily. During the late 1980s and early 1990s the reserve for labor created by Bangkok's economic policy did "help" Thailand build up an export-oriented, labor-intensive industrial sector as well. As we have seen, agricultural policy suppressed household incomes for a large part of the population, and this reduced wage costs. The low wages combined with political and macroeconomic stability, a decent infrastructure, and tax exemptions in turn made Thailand an attractive production base for export companies. But the export sector was largely cordoned off from the rest of the economy, as I realized when I visited Sweden and in the shops there saw all the goods—clothes, interior furnishing articles, and electronic products—that had been manufactured in Thailand. I'd never seen them in Thailand itself; in Bangkok they were unobtainable. Why? Because the export industry confined itself to exports only. Export companies had been localized in special enclaves, known as export zones, where they were exempted from certain taxes and import tariffs on the condition that all their output be exported. They are actually banned from selling to Thai consumers, unless they pay high import tariffs. Often this means such cumbersome calculations and red tape that they'd rather not bother. Sometimes, though, products shipped out by the export companies are then shipped back in: You'll find goods on Bangkok store shelves that were made in Thailand—and imported from Singapore.

If the goal is to improve the lot of the impoverished Thai farmer, the government needs to get out of the way: Quotas must be abolished, tariffs must be slashed, the economy must be deregulated.

* * *

The Brazilianization of Brazil and Thailand is not caused by globalization. If Thailand is better off than Brazil, it is because the economy has, in spite of everything, become more open and less inflated.

Brazil and Thailand were caught not in the globalization trap but in the isolation trap. Their tribulations show why only globalization and markets—deregulation, freer trade, the dissemination of new technology—can save disadvantaged groups from strong, predatory elites. Globalization turns yesterday's victims into tomorrow's winners.

Globalization will not solve all the problems of all developing countries. The gentle breeze of liberalism at the eleventh hour cannot be expected to slough away all the structural, cultural, and social misfortune wrought by 50 years or more of destructive economic policies. But the goalposts are clear—as is the direction in which we need to go.

Critics say Western Europe and the United States are now also in danger of becoming Brazilianized, and that free trade, low inflation, and unrestrained flows of capital will be the nefarious agents of this process. The reality of economic life in countries like Brazil and Thailand casts doubt on the very terms in which such critics have cast the debate. If rich western countries are in fact at risk of being "Brazilianized," we'll have to look elsewhere for the causes.

6. Unfair Trade

In 1993, Siam Cycle, a Thai bicycle factory near Bangkok, was shipping more than 200,000 mountain bikes to the countries of the European Union—mainly to Germany, France, the United Kingdom, and Italy.

A year later, Siam was shipping zero to those markets. "Not one single bicycle," a forlorn marketing manager, Prasit Visedpaitoon, told me.

That's because, in late 1993, the European Commission in Brussels announced that it had begun an anti-dumping investigation of Siam Cycle and other bicycle exporters in Thailand. The mere hint that the Commission might impose punitive tariffs sent European importers lurching for the exit. Their fears were soon confirmed: On top of the regular import duties of 16.6 percent, the Commission slapped another levy of 41.9 percent on the Thai bikes.

For Siam Cycle, the action was an exceptionally hard blow. The company had grown dependent on the European market; 90 percent of its products were exported, almost all to Europe. "We didn't have any other export markets that could compensate the loss of sales to Europe," Prasit admitted. "So we had to reduce the number of employees in the factory from 350 to 200 and completely redirect production and marketing. Now we're targeting only the Thai market." In hindsight, Siam's decision to put all its eggs in one European basket seems foolish. Thai bike makers had every reason to be on guard against Brussels: Their Chinese competitors had already fallen prey to punitive tariffs.

So-called anti-dumping duties are an instrument of trade policy designed to protect European manufacturers from "unfair" (i.e., competitive) foreign competition. Under the EU rules, a product is "dumped" if its export price is lower than the price of a comparable product in the country from which the product is being exported— Thailand, in this case—or if the export price is judged by the Eurocrats to be lower than the production cost. The fact that markets in

Thailand or Bosnia might be a bit different from markets in France or England doesn't get factored into the equation.

For example: In the EU, mountain bikes are a mass product. Volume is large, competition keen. In Thailand, the demand for such a luxury item is much smaller, so higher prices can be charged. Of course, the necessity of making different business decisions in different markets is not entirely unknown to the European enterprises seeking to be immunized from foreign-born competition, nor perhaps even to their co-conspirators on the Commission. At any rate, such economic realities deter neither party. As Disraeli noted, "Protection is not a principle but an expedient."

And so, with the Commission hard on its heels, the bicycle industry has been chased from one country to another, from Taiwan to China to Thailand to . . . the European Union itself. Leif Hellberg, product manager with the Swedish import firm OK Marknadsservice AB, says his company "came very close to doing business with Thailand and Indonesia. We were on the point of placing an order with Siam Cycle. Now we've had to go to suppliers in Germany and Italy." When the Commission stopped the trade in Siamese bicycles, many European importers saw no point in developing a business relationship with manufacturers in Vietnam and India either, even though firms in these nominally unaffected countries could presumably have cashed in on the demise of Siam Cycles.

"That might have worked for a year," says Hellberg, "but the Commission is so wide awake that new duties are added as soon as bicycles start coming in from a new country. Building up the contacts is too expensive. We imported our last Asian bicycle in July 1994."

Anti-dumping measures had been taken against other Asian products too, like color TV sets, computer diskettes, and disposable lighters. In 1997, the following goods were subject to punitive duties in the European Union: shoes (29.1 percent duty), iron and steel (29.3 percent), leather goods (22.9 percent), metal products (44.4 percent), office and computer equipment (19.5 percent), radio, television, and communications (23.2 percent). (Presumably these percentages were pulled out of a hat.)

A single complaint by a European firm nervous over the rough and tumble of an unhampered market is all that is needed to launch an investigation. The EC's 200-page annual anti-dumping report catalogs investigations pertaining to iron from India, Taiwan, South

Africa, Yugoslavia, and Taiwan; "video tapes on reels" from the Republic of Korea; television camera systems and "parts of television camera systems" from the United States and Japan; One Dye Black 1 and One Dye Black 2 from Japan; ammonium nitrate from Lithuania; polyester staple fibers from India; "stainless steel wire having a diameter of less than 1 mm" from India and Korea; "stainless steel wire having a diameter of 1 mm or more" from India and Korea; pipes and tubes from Croatia and the Ukraine; baler twine from Saudi Arabia; insecticide from Denmark; cut-to-length steel plates from France and Italy. You get the idea. Again and again, reduced market share and lower prices are prima facie evidence that a domestic company's been done wrong.

As of early 2000, many of these investigations were still pending. But 156 measures, covering 63 products and 35 countries, were currently in force, including duties on bed linen from Egypt, India, and Pakistan; microdisks from Hong Kong; antibiotics from India; footwear with textile uppers from China and Indonesia; hardboard from Eastern Europe; microwave ovens from China, Malaysia, Korea, and Thailand; monosodium glutamate from Brazil, Vietnam, Korea, and Taiwan; advertising matches from Japan.

Producing ring binder mechanisms seems to be one of the more perilous endeavors one could engage in, if you live in China. One newsletter devoted to EU trading issues blandly reported, in its October 2000 issue, that "anti-dumping duties imposed in January 1997 on imports of ring binder mechanisms from China into the European Union were raised by the EU's Council of Ministers on 29 September. For mechanisms other than those with 17 and 23 rings, the Member States set a single rate of 78.8 percent for Chinese imports and 51.2 percent for China's World Wide Stationery company (32.5 percent in 1997). The separate duties of 10.5 percent for imports from Malaysia were unchanged by the Council." If you can distill the moral logic of treating 23-ring binding mechanisms differently from 22-ring binding mechanisms, you're a wiser man than I am.

There is also an odd quota affecting non-human dolls originating in China, which resulted in half of one particular shipment being turned back at the European border. Why? Well, they were "Star Trek" action figures, and half represented Captain Kirk, half Mr. Spock. Kirk is human. Spock, of course, is Vulcan—well, half-Vul-

31

can, if you want to get technical. The doll, for its part, is mostly just plastic. (Did somebody say "Beam me out of here"?)

Who suffers when the anti-dumping edicts sprout in Brussels? In the first instance, of course, the foreign firms and their employees. In the second instance, European consumers, importers, and trading companies. In the third instance, home-grown exporters—or any other company that makes use of imported components. The EU's habit of slapping duties on Asian electronic gadgets—memory circuits from South Korea, for example—has put EU-based companies like cell phone makers Ericsson and Nokia at a competitive disadvantage. "We believe that there is a larger risk for the EU in keeping the duties than in abolishing them," says Nina Norén at Ericsson's information department. If competitive pressure and economic options promote rather than preclude economic progress, she's right.

Europe, of course, is not alone in deploying arbitrary and punitive duties. The United States can be just as vigorous in penalizing goods of foreign origin, notwithstanding its sometimes vigorous free-trade rhetoric. As can Asia. And the international organization that is supposed to grease the skids of international trade may be running off the rails.

7. The WTO Trap

In late November of 1999, globalized soldiers of anti-globalization—some of whom had posted their operational blueprints on the Internet—descended as a great mass on the city of Seattle, Washington. Like the trade delegates flying in from around the globe, they had come in anticipation of the annual meeting of the World Trade Organization.

The 50,000 or so converging protesters ranged from youthful ski-masked rebels scavenging for a cause to union activists, environmentalists, and champions of animal rights. Not all the protesters had the same axe to grind. Several hundred supporters of Falun Gong demonstrated peacefully to call attention to China's persecution of that group. There were even a few gray-suited conservatives on hand to take issue with illiberal aspects of WTO trade rules and organizational policy. But the main theme of the demonstrations was anti-liberalization, anti-globalization, anti-trade.

The anti-capitalist contingents were out in full force on the inaugural day of the proceedings. Despite all the loud advance warning, authorities seemed blindsided. Seattle police could not establish a safe route between the Convention Center and the Paramount Theatre just a few blocks away, where opening ceremonies were scheduled. While most of the protesters were peaceful—to the extent that blocking traffic and preventing people from going where they want to go is peaceful—the violence and vandalism that did occur, and which took law enforcement by surprise, had been plotted well in advance. From atop a bus barricade, a French animal rights activist delivered a rousing condemnation of McDonald's, global symbol of corporate enterprise unbound. The speechifying was followed immediately by a "spontaneous" looting of a downtown McDonald's as crowds chanted anti-capitalist slogans. Other bouts of "spontaneous" vandalism were also committed simultaneously, as instigators made sure that crowds of more peaceful demonstrators were on hand to serve as buffers between themselves and the police. Vandals smashed windows up and down a retail corridor of the downtown area. Two Starbucks shops were looted and destroyed. For their own safety, delegates were confined in the Convention Center. As the day wore on, Seattle's mayor declared a state of civil emergency. Only by early morning did authorities get the situation under control.

The next few days saw more of the same. In the end, the year's round of trade meetings had accomplished little—but not because of the protesters. At least, not directly.

In 1998 the multilateral negotiating process had celebrated its 50th anniversary. A new round of negotiations for greater free trade was to begin January 1, 2000, with a kickoff a month earlier in conjunction with the ill-fated summit meeting in Seattle. But the Millennium Round never happened, primarily because the key nations—the United States and the European Union—could not agree on the agenda. Efforts are now under way to launch a new negotiating round, and chances may be a bit better under a Bush administration.

But is that the right path to take? Not necessarily. Though multilateral trade policy clearly arouses widespread revulsion, no one seems disposed to alter the process. As long as not only the professional activists but also the general public view the liberalization process as little more than logrolling between faceless bureaucrats and devious politicians, trade liberalization will increasingly lack political legitimacy. Institutionalized multilateralism is at risk of becoming a political dead end—if it isn't already.

Just the same, many want to expand the WTO's power and responsibilities; sometimes the demands clash. Companies and governments, especially in Europe, want the trade organization to regulate states' ability to hamper the investment opportunities of foreign companies. Meanwhile, environmentalist organizations and unions want WTO rules to take environmental and working conditions of trading partners into account, to prevent the environmental and social "dumping" that allegedly take place when producers flee to countries where workers and the environment are least protected.

By July 1999, a petition against the WTO had garnered the signatures of more than 700 organizations. The motley alliance included the Church of Sweden and the French Ligue Communiste Revolutionnaire, the Norwegian Wildlife Protection Association, the American Anarchism Now! and consumer rights organizations from Japan to Venezuela. According to their petition, in the first few years of its existence the WTO "contributed to the concentration of wealth in the hands of the rich few." The sole beneficiaries of free trade are transnational corporations, raking it in "at the expense of" national economies, workers, farmers, and the environment. The declaration describes the rules and procedures of WTO as undemocratic, opaque, and unaccountable.

The petitioners conclude that a moratorium must be imposed on the WTO regime: No new liberalization measures until the existing system is reviewed comprehensively and in depth for the WTO's "impact on marginalized communities, development, democracy, environment, health, human rights, labor rights and the rights of women and children." The review would "provide an opportunity for society to change course and develop an alternative, humane and sustainable international system of trade and investment relations." The compatibility of such an "alternative system" with *free* trade is of course hard to imagine—freedom being regarded as the arch defect of the present system.

Skeptics of free trade may have a point when they say that the workings of the WTO lack transparency and accountability—but not when they say that those workings are undemocratic. The opacity and unaccountability—to the degree they exist—may spring rather from an *excess* of democracy. The WTO is so democratic, it has become unwieldy. It is akin to a coalition government comprising of more than 130 different parties. Governing by consensus means that any member nation can veto any substantive decision. That explains the need for secret negotiations. But it's also a good prescription for not getting anything done, notwithstanding the façade of hectic and inscrutable activity.

To allay distrust and suspicion of the WTO, what the organization needs is not "democratizing," but some influential friends who are willing to speak openly and clearly about the benefits of free trade. But the governments of member countries often want the WTO to appear mighty even when it is not. It makes for a convenient scapegoat when national governments are suffering the economic consequences of their own political failings, in the form of rising unemployment, widening economic inequality, and the like. It is nice not to have to set forth honest but unpopular political arguments. One need only complain about how one's hands are tied by the big bad WTO.

When, late in his administration, Bill Clinton decided to veto a bill that would have imposed new quotas on foreign steel imports, he did not make the case that the law should be vetoed because it was bad for Americans (who would have to pay higher prices for their cars), or because it would be bad for the many crisis-prone countries for which export restrictions could easily turn recession into full-blown depression. Instead, he stressed the fact that the bill would breach WTO law.

The sponsors of "A Citizen's Guide to the World Trade Organization," a brochure published by the Working Group on the WTO/MAI in July 1999, include the Teamsters, the United Steelworkers of America, the environmentalist organization Friends of the Earth, and consumer rights activist Ralph Nader's group Public Citizen. On the cover the WTO is represented as an enormous dinosaur, "GATTzilla," a creature that totes a barrel of DDT under one arm, crushes the U.S. Congress underfoot, and gobbles up the earth. Free trade—as symbolized by the WTO—is thus presented as a mortal threat to the environment and democracy.

This stark demagogy meshes all too well with the anti-capitalist ideology of less respectable constellations. The British National Party, the extreme right-wing nationalist party in Britain, seeks to revive British industry by excluding imports. Sweden's neo-Nazi National Socialist Front has as the foundation stone of its policies the reinstatement of Sweden's traditional industries, "through a redirection of trade policy in favor of the greatest possible self-sufficiency and a reversion to ecological agriculture." Right on key with the rallying cry of the Seattle protests that trade should be "local not global."

But this is not a movement only of Naderites and nationalist fringes. The critics of WTO and free trade have many friends in the establishment. The demands of unions and environmentalists helped make it politically possible—in the name of "globalization with a human face"—for an intermittently pro-trade Clinton administration to stop imports from countries with inferior safeguards for workers and the environment. Whether world leaders will be less squishy on such matters now that George W. Bush is in the saddle remains to be seen. One hopeful sign is the suggestion of Pascal Lamy, the European Commission's trade czar, that the EU should rethink its stance on trade before undertaking a new WTO round, particularly when it comes to labor standards and the like—a hint that the protectionist agenda may be growing less tenable, or at least more debatable.

With the failure of the Millennium Round, the WTO has been reduced from a forum for broad negotiations on trade issues to an international court of law in trade matters. In past years the WTO and its predecessor, the General Agreement on Tariffs and Trade (GATT), have been able to deliberate and act in silence. But no longer. In Seattle thousands of activists demonstrated and exerted other kinds of pressure to promote their "alternative" agenda. While the actions of the brick-throwers may speak for but a tiny minority, the opinions of those brick-throwers speak for many.

Genuinely pro-trade politicians and opinion leaders can rescue free trade from the WTO trap by aggressively advocating unilateral liberalization. What is needed is not more logrolling by elitist associations like the WTO, but an open, straightforward trade policy that is not so easy for the protectionists and demagogues to smear.

8. Good Times, Bad Policy

The goings-on in Seattle may have seemed alien to the American spirit. But the protestors' message, if not their methods, resonates widely among Americans.

Protectionists like to speak of the treason of the elites. Economic and political leaders, we are told, have been seduced by the great god Market; they're all market fundamentalists now. Their alleged project is said to be as utopian as its Marxist-Leninist precursor ever was—and as indifferent to the impact of utopianism on ordinary people. They are propelling, willy-nilly, a "race to the bottom."

Such anti-elitist talk is especially the rage in the United States. For a couple of presidential election cycles it was a major vote-getting theme for billionaire-turned-candidate Ross Perot as well as for commentator-turned-candidate Pat Buchanan. Buchanan calls his latest book *The Great Betrayal;* its thesis is that the elites have greatly betrayed ordinary folk by embracing free trade and globalization—which are "killing America" by toppling traditional industries and rending the traditional fabric of society. A return to classical trade protectionism is the only way the country can heal its social wounds and bridge its economic gaps. Radical economic de-globalization is essential if America is to recover her soul. The friends of free trade are the enemies of America.

But Buchanan vastly exaggerates his opposition. Few members of the economic and political elite in the United States—or in the western world overall—are principled advocates of liberal economic policy. In fact, free trade has not benefited from one single consistent defender in American politics. Critics, on the other hand, abound, on both the left and the right.

Buchanan is seen as right-wing. On the left, there's Richard Gephardt, leader of the Democratic Party in the House of Representatives, who has spearheaded campaigns against the North American Free Trade Agreement (NAFTA), trade with China, and fast track. He wants, he says, not free trade, but *fair* trade. The foremost symptom of unfair trade, he believes, is America's trade deficit.

The solution? Punish countries that do not share American values (or at any rate, can't afford to pay for them). In *An Even Better Place*, Gephardt complains that while Americans have succeeded in broadening the trade agenda, they haven't yet managed to elevate human rights, worker rights, and environmental protection to the status of permanent, central elements of United States negotiating strategy. And only when that's been done can the United States hope to craft a trade strategy that effectively promotes high and rising living standards all over the world. He thus shares the mind-set of an organization of student activists that emerged out of the WTO protests, the Davis Working Group on Globalization, which promotes "fair trade" coffee—brands certifiably produced by workers making a "fair" wage. But as a matter of practical politics, Gephardt is a lot more worried about protecting workers in the United States than improving the lot of workers overseas.

Like many Americans—and more than a few Europeans—Gephardt and Buchanan believe that present-day trade between countries has triggered a "race to the bottom," a situation where competition is forcing companies to send investment and production to places where wages and taxes are lowest and environment protection worst, at the expense of economic well-being. Although Haiti, Rwanda, and Murmansk are not exactly investment hot spots, this idea is implicitly accepted in many quarters.

Somebody will doubtless respond to all this that it makes little difference what the likes of Buchanan and Gephardt think. Union influence is waning in the new economy, and neither Buchanan nor Gephardt will ever enjoy broad enough appeal to be president of the United States.

But union votes still mean a great deal to American politicians, and the left-right protectionist alliance has its adjutants and followers among opinion-molders and the public. And if you can gain votes with populist appeals—for example, from disaffected workers in low-skilled jobs or Christian fundamentalists who disapprove of trading with China—without alienating any other important group of voters, then populist protectionism may well carry the day.

A *Wall Street Journal*/NBC News Survey conducted between April 29 and May 1, 2000, showed that 48 percent of Americans believe that foreign trade is "bad for the U.S. economy, as cheap imports hurt wages and cost jobs." Only 34 percent believe that foreign trade is good for the United States economy, creating jobs and spurring growth. And contrary to Buchanan, the country's elites have also become increasingly protectionist in recent years. In 1994 only 20 percent of those ranked among the political, economic, and media leaders of the United States felt that import duties should be raised. Four years later, no less than 34 percent were advocating higher tariff walls. Despite record-low unemployment, record-low inflation, rapid economic growth, and rising wages and stock values.

But it may be this very prosperity that, in America, helps make an economically destructive trade policy possible.

"It is only in times of prosperity that you can pursue an economically expensive policy; that's when you can afford it," says Gary Jacobson, professor of political science at the University of California, San Diego. "Buchanan may never become president, but other politicians are taking up his position to win votes. There is a deep vein of anti-elitism in the United States, and many people regard free trade as an elite project foisted on America by Wall Street, intellectuals, and Washington bureaucrats. The general public has not yet realized the important role of international trade in the economy. They do not realize how many jobs depend on exports or how low consumer prices depend on imports."

Considering (1) the meager support which free trade enjoys in public opinion and (2) the relatively low economic cost of bad trade policy in good economic times, it is not very surprising that in recent years free trade has had to take a back seat in the U.S. Congress. A study of congressional voting behavior in 1997 and 1998 showed that only about 6 percent of members could be described as firm and consistent free traders (in the sense of taking a stand for free trade and against various forms of trade subsidization), a fact reflected in a long succession of reverses for free trade. One sign of the times was President Clinton's inability to renew the fast track authority that expired in 1994 and which was enjoyed by previous presidents.

Fast track means that Congress is obliged to vote up or down on trade agreements negotiated by the administration with other countries; it cannot propose any amendments. The president and his ministers can engage in trade negotiations without fast track, but in practice it is hard to reach settlement when those on the other side of the negotiating table know that what they're hammering out can be easily obstructed or derailed by the American legislature.

President Clinton's vision of international trade was long embattled on both sides of the aisle. On the Democratic side, support for free trade had receded rapidly in the wake of the battle for North American Free Trade Agreement, which Clinton pushed through early in his administration and which had provoked the bitter opposition of unions and environmentalists, key Democratic supporters. For the remainder of his tenure, Clinton did not dare make an issue of free trade with the hard-core Democrats and their constituents. (The AFL-CIO, for example, was especially determined to put a stop to fast track.) Clinton's reluctance to expend political capital on free trade meant, for one thing, that he waited almost a year to apply for a renewal of fast track authority after his big election victory in 1996. Some of the opposition to fast track did originate in pro-trade sentiment: Republicans especially, but a few Democrats too, oppose Clinton's idea of international trade agreements being cluttered with environmental and labor policy norms.

The defeat of fast track was only one American-sponsored setback for free trade. The United States has also obstructed China's entry into the World Trade Organization. In the spring of 1999 China and the United States held negotiations to define the terms on which the United States could endorse China's application. A preliminary settlement was reached, but President Clinton did not present the agreement to the Congress; he didn't want to offend the unions. The Republican majority in Congress had such a hearty dislike of Clinton that they were reluctant to contribute to his triumphs of trade policy. And some did believe that trade with China might help perpetuate repressive policies (although others may have adopted that moral stance disingenuously). So freer trade with China had to be deferred, and the prospect became even more uncertain when American planes mistakenly bombed the Chinese Embassy in Belgrade, further weakening the position of Beijing's pro-reform politicians. But the bill finally did pass in 2000.

The United States dropped the ball elsewhere in Asia and the Pacific too. In 1997, the United States pushed for a rapid liberalization of trade by the members of the regional organization Asia-Pacific Economic Cooperation (APEC). But a couple of years later the negotiations fizzled and the job was turned over to the WTO. According to Pierre G. Goad, economic correspondent for the respected *Far Eastern Economic Review*, the Clinton administration was perhaps the biggest obstacle to progress with respect to both China and APEC—not, as is commonly supposed, mercantilist Asians.

Free trade has also been damaged by a wide range of American restrictions, ranging from special trade sanctions on countries that do not respect religious liberty to fat protective tariffs on "unfair" steel and other imports. Steve Chapman, of the *Chicago Tribune*, observed that in 1999 alone, the Commerce Department

> found dumping by steelmakers in Germany, France, South Korea, Italy, Japan, Mexico, Taiwan, Great Britain, Russia, and Brazil—which suggests that everyone is out of step but us. This is no accident. The law is written in such a way that it outlaws all sorts of normal commercial behavior. So foreign companies that engage in such behavior can expect to be keelhauled for doing things that are perfectly legal and praiseworthy when American firms conducting business at home do them.

Duties set on illegally dumped goods average about 45 percent, and 98 percent of complaints are upheld. Oil companies have tried to get in on the action too. Before the latest price hikes, a group of American domestic oil industries formed a group called Save Domestic Oil to complain that Saudi Arabia and three other countries were "dumping" petroleum on the American market at unchivalrously low prices. The Commerce Department dismissed the complaint, not so much on the merits or lack thereof, but because not enough oil companies had joined in.

Domestic pistachio farmers—specifically, the Iranian expatriates who dominate the U.S. pistachio market—have had an easier time of it. In March of 2000 it appeared that a 13-year-old ban on Iranian nuts and some other products was finally being lifted. But with the Commerce Department still saving us from "dumped" Iranian pistachios with duties of 283 percent for raw Iranian pistachio nuts, 318 percent for roasted ones, opening the domestic market remains a hard nut to crack.

Other efforts at liberalization have also either fallen by the wayside or been disgracefully delayed. Until 2000, legislation aimed at lowering American duties on imports from nearly 30 countries in the West Indies and Central America was defeated in no small measure thanks to the lobbying of Fruit of the Loom, an American manufacturer of underwear. It is hard to imagine a narrower vested interest than the American underwear industry—maybe the American Iranian expatriate pistachio industry would qualify—but like other interest groups in the United States, the underwear people have substantial political clout with Congress, enough to dump legislation which would help millions of people in abjectly poor countries like Haiti and the Dominican Republic to help themselves through trade with the United States. Now that the bill has finally been passed, they have a better chance.

The list goes on, as do the pitched battles. Time and time again, American politicians claim that no one is as determined as they to tear down protectionist barriers—even as they impose new special protections for domestic industry. Those who allege that American politicians pray to the great god Market and regard the liberal economist and philosopher Hayek as its prophet have never troubled to scrutinize the actual legislative behavior of these politicians. They do have some regard for the concept, but they're not afraid to cheat on it, either. Like policymakers everywhere, they're often more inclined to heed powerful vested interests than their own common sense or purported ideological convictions. If we're lucky, the pragmatic calculus will move more and more in the direction of free trade. But there's no guarantee.

The *New York Times* columnist Thomas Friedman has argued that globalization is the definitive political issue of the future. Ideological fire will not be consumed by the struggle between right and left but between globalists and anti-globalists, between those who welcome and those who fear economic openness. Perhaps that's so in other countries, but it does not appear to be so in the United States. In America, the political establishment appears to have rallied round a politically pragmatic compromise between globalism and isolationism. In his State of the Union Address of 1999, Bill Clinton opined that trade issues had divided Americans for too long, and that

> we have to find a common ground on which business and workers and environmentalists and farmers and government can stand together.... Now that the world economy is becoming more and more integrated, we have to do in the world what we spent the better part of this century doing here at home. We have got to put a human face on the global economy.

These days you can't sell the Luddite message that machinery and computers ought to be smashed to save the jobs of yesteryear, at any rate not in America. Anyone who wants to hammer the computers, unplug the phones, and yank the electric lights is an acknowledged reactionary. What's politically correct now is hammering trade to protect "welfare." In the land of the free, can this new reactionary theology, this Third Way, long endure? Alas, it might.

9. Trading Up

You can't build a an automobile economy on bicycle wages, warned Walter Reuther, former president of the United Auto Workers, during a visit to Japan.

The idea harks back to Henry Ford, who paid his workers so well that they could afford to buy Ford cars. Reuther was pointing out that workers in the Japanese motor factories could not afford to buy the cars they were producing—they cycled to work. Meanwhile, workers at the less-productive American motor companies, which a decade or so later would lose market share to the Japanese assault, naturally drove to work. The Japanese were building their automobile economy mostly by exporting to the United States and Europe. If they wanted an automobile economy, they'd have to start hiking the wages of Japanese workers so the Japanese workers could buy the Japanese cars too.

Not the strongest of arguments, perhaps. Ford's motive was to bid away the best workers and improve his company's performance and profitability, not create a demand from scratch—the market for newly cheap automobiles would have been poor indeed had it been confined to Ford's employees! But the memory of Henry Ford's salary hike is still being regularly deployed to rationalize trade barriers. Spearheaded by John J. Sweeney of the AFL-CIO, union leaders constantly evoke Reuther's aphorism when calling for new forms of protectionism, like the social clauses in trade agreements aimed, allegedly, at putting a stop to the "Nike economy." The expression refers to the trendy sneaker designed and marketed by well-paid Americans but manufactured by low-paid workers from Mexico to Vietnam. It is certainly true that the young women stitching Nikes in Thailand and China can't afford to jog to work in Nike's latest, most expensive model. It is even true that, by Western European standards, their wages are terribly low. But how would Western protectionism help them? It might, of course, help American union workers keep their current jobs at their current wages, without having to bother beating foreign competitors.

While some may be a tad disingenuous in their push for "fair trade," others are doubtless sincere. But as Jagdish Bhagwati, professor of economics at Columbia University, has noted, imposing international limits to trade to promote moral or environmental concerns amounts to a kind of colonialism. Its principle is "might makes right," with the larger, richer, most powerful countries lording it over the not-so-rich and not-so-powerful ones. The United States can impose trade sanctions against India if Indian fishermen are nasty to dolphins, but India cannot realistically bar trade with the United States if Americans are nasty to cows. Similarly, the United States can punish Norway if Norwegians do not want to eat gene-manipulated beef, but Norway cannot realistically punish the United States if U.S. labor law is less generous toward union interests than Norwegian labor law. Are contentious issues of governance—about which there is rarely consensus even within the boundaries of a particular country—really to be settled by trade clauses, rather than domestic politics and persuasion?

Bhagwati suggests that, instead, we accept as a basic tenet of trade policy that ethical choices must be made primarily by the producers and consumers themselves—not by politicians and bureaucrats acting in their name. In any case, "ethical" trade restrictions usually don't achieve what they set out to achieve, if they ever do. The key causes of poor labor and environmental standards are poverty and despotism, and there is little that yet another bout of protectionism can do to alleviate poverty or foster freedom and democracy in countries like China, Pakistan, and Burma. In fact, trying to promote "core labor standards" via tariff barriers may well accomplish the opposite of its intention.

Keith E. Maskus, an economist at the University of Colorado, has studied the issue of core labor standards for the World Bank. He concludes that attempts to stop so-called "social dumping" from poor nations pose a "real and serious risk" to the well-being of some of the most vulnerable members of Third World societies. "The celebrated French ban of soccer balls sewn in Pakistan for the World Cup in 1998 resulted in significant dislocation of children from employment. Those who tracked them found that a large proportion ended up begging and/or in prostitution," Maskus told me. Shutting down a non-optimal opportunity does not thereby install a better one in its place.

Of all the world's child workers, less than 5 percent labor in export industries. That means that even if trade with industries that hire children were banned altogether, only a very small number of the world's child laborers would be helped—if such a ban would help at all. To close the door to exports to countries such as Pakistan and India, where child labor is common, might be a symbolically forceful action in some eyes. But how morally satisfying could it be, if the main effect is to harm the weakest of the weak?

"If it were possible to implement surgically precise sanctions aimed at particular products we might anticipate some willingness to improve standards," says Maskus. "But such precision is impossible; rather, we will see the monstrosity of antidumping applied to wide swaths of labor-intensive products. Given the reliance of such manufactures on export sales, the potential risks for workers in developing countries are indeed large."

One fear is that trade with countries with lower labor standards will engender loss of jobs back home. But in general, poor labor standards are a competitive *disadvantage* to an economy—or result from deeper problems that hamper the economy. The race to the bottom is a figment of imagination: It is not, after all, countries with the worst human rights records that top the annual rankings of national competitiveness. And it is certainly not the countries with the lowest wages and least protection for workers that dominate export markets or attract the lion's share of foreign direct investment.

This is hardly surprising. National leaders who pay scant attention to the rights of workers are unlikely to pay much attention to a host of other important civic protections either: private property rights, freedom of the press, the rule of law, etc. Treating labor badly—by banning the right to organize, for example—is thus only one symptomatic thread of a skein of policies that can smother economic development in totalitarian or authoritarian regimes. It's not only morally repugnant, it is also likely to harm the country's export potential and, thus, the economic well-being of its citizens. Governments that recognize legitimate social interests are more likely to respect private property and contracts. This makes for less arbitrary government, more predictable rules, and a better climate for investment and innovation.

How can the political structures of developing countries be made more open and democratic? Should democratic nations trade at all with authoritarian states, or would doing so be morally repugnant? Can economic isolation force dastardly regimes to reform? Can it eliminate child labor?

When pondering such questions it should be kept in mind that almost all countries that are today prosperous and democratic were once poor and undemocratic. Increased international trade is one of the factors that has led to rising prosperity—and to rising demands for political openness. In recent years the process has been evident in such Asian nations as South Korea, Taiwan, the Philippines, Thailand, and Indonesia.

Concerns about child labor are legitimate, and much can be done to combat child labor outside the realm of trade policy. International aid helps finance the schooling of millions of working children. But such ad hoc assistance can be only part of the solution. The core dilemma is that many countries pursue economic policies that make investing in education an unprofitable proposition. If poor families are to be persuaded of the value of education, they must see that schooling leads to relatively well-paid jobs. Free trade and economic growth are what create such jobs. Economic sanctions don't.

What rich countries can do to help is dismantle trade barriers. Both the EU and the United States levy lower tariffs on unprocessed goods from the developing world than they do on processed goods. As a result, fewer jobs for educated youths are created than would otherwise be possible. And this, in turn, contributes to the social situation that paves the way for exploitation of child labor. Private pressure by companies that trade overseas can also help: "U.S. companies that contract their work overseas [including Nike] have found it in their interest to be sensitive to worker-abuse charges," the *Christian Science Monitor* reported early in 2001. "By insisting on improved conditions in factories, the firms find the better-treated workers often are more productive."

What about trading with citizens of the most repugnant kinds of regimes, like communist China? Critics often complain that the policy of "engagement" with China hasn't worked, noting the persistence of widespread political repression—against minorities, labor activists, political organizers, workers, writers and intellectuals, members of Falun Gong, etc. But it would be naïve to expect that more fully integrating China into the global economy must result in an immediate political thaw. History suggests that communist governments almost never adapt and reform—they collapse. The policy of engagement must therefore be judged over the long haul.

The years of Mao are over. China's government is no longer attempting the wholesale reconstruction of society; instead it is fighting a rearguard action to preserve the status quo. And no matter how hard Chinese officials try, they have been unable to squelch entirely the political changes that economic liberalization has wrought, whether in the form of the student protests in Tianamen Square or the peaceful meditative exercises of the Falun Gong. These days the outside world has a much better idea of what happens in China—as a direct consequence of the social and political dynamics resulting from increased economic openness and rising prosperity. The Chinese people, for their part, are learning much more about the outside world and the alternatives to their own system. If their government hopes to keep reaping the benefits of economic liberalization, it can't root out every element of capitalist reform it has permitted since the 1980s. And if it does try to turn back the clock, simmering discontent could become explosive.

So the policy of engagement may be working: Albeit slowly and unpredictably, China is approaching the day when it will no longer be ruled by "the butchers of Beijing."

When one considers the poor results of economic sanctions against Cuba, Libya, Iraq, North Korea, and Burma, it seems clear that economic isolation of authoritarian regimes rarely if ever leads to impressive social and political advances. Free trade is the only truly fair trade. The best thing rich countries can do to make brutish regimes in faraway places less nasty and more short-lived is to help their citizens gain access to globalized information, technologies, and markets. Give nations and their peoples a stake in international trade, and thus a stake in the capitalist and liberal values that will enable their economies to be more competitive, their lives to be better.

10. Errors of the Free Traders

Advocates of free trade do not always present their ideas in the most persuasive way. For example, they often claim that freer trade will create *more* jobs, when in fact free trade creates *better* jobs, more productive jobs—higher-paid jobs. (It is conceivable that in a poor economy, everyone could be slogging away 12 hours a day, achieving little more than subsistence.) Nor, as is often intimated, will the domestic "losers" of an international economic competition be automatically and immediately awarded the new, better jobs that trade makes possible. So when growing international trade results in certain industries or jobs being shipped overseas, idealized pictures of free trade strike the victims as a mockery.

Champions of free trade also tend to stress that free trade spurs *exports*, as if exports were all that mattered. In many countries, trade deficits—a state of affairs in which more goods are imported than exported—are regarded as something evil, something to be repaired, while trade surpluses are deemed the supreme blessing. The trade balance is thus taken as prima facie evidence of economic superiority or inferiority. But exports and imports are two sides of the same coin. They refer to transactions the like of which take place in domestic markets every day, transactions in which *both* participants in the transaction expect to benefit (else they would not participate in the exchange to begin with). Trade between different countries is simply made up of particular trades between particular individuals, and each specific trade is perfectly "balanced" as soon as it is successfully completed.

As a consumer, I would love it if all manner of imports were "dumped" in my lap at exorbitantly low prices. A pair of shoes imported from overseas is just as good for my feet as the same pair from a domestic firm: If the imported shoe is cheaper, all the better. (The overseas shoemaker, of course, also benefits from his ability to profitably supply that cheaper product to me; and neither he nor his employees would be helped by losing the chance to conduct so-called "unfair" trade with me.) After all, production is not an end in itself. I produce so that I can consume—buy textbooks, take care of my family, go on vacation, etc.

Cheaper imports also benefit me as a producer. First, because my now-lower costs as a consumer leave me with more capital to produce with. Second, because not all of the cheaper imports will be consumer goods. If I am a manufacturer of electronics, cheaper microchips or casings from overseas allow me to lower my production costs directly—giving me a better chance to compete globally. And to hire more people!

Of course, my success as a competitor is not guaranteed, and it may be very inconvenient to have to face a smart new competitor on the international horizon. But the challenges of competition are inherent in the market process. And I'm better off adjusting to competition than forsaking the benefits of division of labor and trade altogether.

Yet a progressive shutting down of the market is exactly the result to which protective tariffs must lead, if the logic of protectionism to "save jobs" is followed to its natural conclusion. After all, the same rationale of "saving jobs" that is evoked when a U.S. firm faces tough competition from Mexico or Taiwan also applies when a Wisconsin firm faces tough competition from an Idaho firm, or from a Wisconsin firm in another town or across the street. No one could ever make a move to improve economic life if every time he had the means of doing so, an already-existing firm could stop him from bringing those improvements to market.

It is just not the case that an economy will grind to a halt—all jobs and production flowing south or east—if companies must contend with competition from abroad. There is no "giant sucking sound" that depletes an advanced economy of resources whenever it faces competition from abroad. What happens when domestic producers are outdone by foreign producers is only that the former are now obliged to shift their efforts from lines in which they do not enjoy an advantage over foreign firms, to lines in which they do enjoy an advantage.

It should be noted that even if a particular economy enjoys an absolute advantage in producing every kind of good—hardly the case—that would still be no general blow to any of its less advantaged trading partners. In each country, production would flow into the lines in which producers enjoy the *comparative* advantage. If producers are allowed to react to circumstances freely, their net productivity would only increase over time.

The principle of comparative advantage is that you are better off doing what you do best (most productively) and letting others do the rest, even if you have the ability to do *everything* better. Consider, for example, the case of an executive and his secretary. An executive may well be more proficient at every task he now assigns to the secretary: He may type faster, take more legible shorthand, be able to screen calls more definitively, etc. In other words, he may enjoy an *absolute* advantage in skill and knowledge in every category. Yet he does not do his secretary's job in addition to his own. Why not? Because he can do something very productively that his secretary cannot do at all—"make million-dollar deals," let us say. As things stand now, he pays his secretary $50,000 a year to run his office while he makes $10,000,000 a year doing ten million-dollar deals a year. If he took over his secretary's job, he could do it in half the time. But he would be able to do only five million-dollar deals a year. Losing $5,000,000 a year in order to save $50,000 a year is not a good economic decision.

Broomstick manufacturers in South Texas may be thrown out of work if broomsticks can now suddenly be imported from Mexico— where broomsticks can be produced, perhaps, at half the cost. But that does not mean the former employees of the South Texas broomstick company now have no choice but to tramp to the unemployment office. Maybe they can make furniture that America's neighbors to the south are not able to produce, or only very expensively, or only with lower quality. And even if the American economy enjoys an absolute advantage over Mexico in making broomsticks, American workers might be more productive still in making cars or computers, or some other good, or perhaps just a different kind of broomstick. In that case, once Mexico is allowed to send its broomsticks to America, American broomstick makers may still ultimately lose their jobs as businesses shift resources to more profitable endeavors—or as workers voluntarily forsake their careers in broomstick manufacture for higher-paying non-broomstick work.

International trade—and trade per se—encourages people to seek the relatively more productive lines into which their efforts can flow. There is no knowing in advance how competition will sort things

out. But we can know that economies will be more robust and productive overall if that sorting out is allowed to take place without
hindrance—if labor, materials, and other resources are allowed to be
continually bid away to relatively more productive uses. Competition is "unfair" only from the perspective of those who feel they have
an unalienable right to rest on their laurels—even when that means
crimping the choices and prospects of everyone else.

If the theoretical defense of free trade often leaves much to be de-
sired, so does its practical implementation. Like Europe, the United
States generally tries to free up world trade through national negotiations within the GATT and the WTO, and regional initiatives like
NAFTA. This method has its shortcomings. Above all, it means that
the negotiators regard duties and regulations in restraint of trade as
crown jewels. When a deal is reached, the crown jewels are discarded. With these kinds of contradictory messages, no wonder
people are skeptical about liberalization!

Unilateral unshackling of trade would be a better bet both economically and politically. The leaders of each country should shout
the message: "We are abolishing trade barriers because it is good for
us, whatever other people do!" And their respective economies
would reap immediate gains as a result. The present modus
operandi—endless negotiations over the swapping of crown jewels—muddies the waters, obscuring the fact that "free trade" is not a
conspiracy of the elites huddling behind closed doors but a matter of
enlightened self-interest.

Objectivity is one thing. Politics is another. Free trade with Asia,
Latin America, and Eastern Europe arouses indignation in Western
circles because of the threat to certain kinds of western job opportunities. Relatively unskilled, unionized workers in traditional male-
dominated jobs especially feel the pinch, which is why imports of
cars from bicycle countries and imports of Nikes from plastic sandal
societies seem so menacing to them. But the only solution is not
economic stasis but economic advancement.

The tactical errors of the free traders—and the demagogic might of
allegations of "unfair" competition—are reflected in public opinion.
A 1998 opinion poll published by *The Economist* showed that a plu-
rality of respondents in the United States, Britain, France, Italy,
Australia, and Russia believe that protectionism does more to promote prosperity in their country than free trade. Later polling by the

Program on International Policy Attitudes at the University of Maryland showed that although Americans broadly favor international trade, or claim to, many have also heard the cries for "fair trade" and want their globalization with heavy doses of labor and environmental protections.

Allowing economies to adjust to changing conditions does have costs. But in the long run, stasis costs even more. The domestic economy of the United States—which, despite the prevalence of protectionist sentiment, is still freer than many in the west—shows that such adjustment is possible.

* * *

In June 1999 I spoke with Tom Still, political editor of the *Wisconsin State Journal* in Madison, Wisconsin. Wisconsin is traditionally dominated by agriculture and heavy industry. A few decades ago the state boasted 160 automobile factories; today, not one remains. I asked Still what political issues Wisconsin voters would be most concerned about over the next few years. Tax relief topped his list. (Both Republicans and Democrats advocate tax cuts, but cannot agree on how to structure them.) Next was medical reform—health insurance and care for the elderly.

Third was agricultural policy: Thousands of farms are going bankrupt. Perhaps that fate could have been avoided if it were easier to export agricultural products to Europe. The forcible setting aside of farmland in the state also gives rise to another controversial political question: How much land—and which land—should the state purchase in order to preserve the original environment?

By contrast, Still does *not* believe that "exports of industrial jobs" will be an important issue. "Manufacturing industries in Wisconsin have done very well indeed in the past 12 years," he says. "True, some people believe that we are losing job opportunities to other parts of the world, and that's an easy question to be demagogic about, but the reality is different. Milwaukee has recovered from the heavy job losses in the manufacturing industry. Today there are more industrial jobs in Milwaukee than there were 20 years ago." That transition might have been foiled had politicians sought to protect the old industrial jobs at all costs. Instead, markets were largely allowed to adapt, to discover new and more productive enterprises.

The descendants of the Scandinavian immigrants who made their way to this state a hundred years ago and founded towns with names like Stockholm and Lund are better off today than they have been for a very long time. Admittedly, Wisconsin is not a high-tech, sun-drenched Silicon Valley. Neither Milwaukee nor Madison, the capital, can compete with the hot spots of the new economy in Seattle, Austin, Dallas, San Jose, or San Diego. But even so, there is no mistaking the state's prosperity. Unemployment is low. Between 1987 and 1997 the number of people on welfare fell by 67 per cent. The number of poor fell by nearly 12 per cent.

Wisconsin reflects the prosperity of middle America generally. A survey by the Pew Research Center in June 1999 showed that Americans are for the most part satisfied with the communities they live in. About two-thirds of respondents believe their part of the country is an "excellent or very good place to live," up from 56 percent two years earlier. Similarly, 35 percent—an increase of 10 percentage units—felt that "people like themselves can play an important part in improving the community they live in." Although economic confidence quavered a bit when signs of economic slowing appeared in 2001, it seems clear that the United States is by no means mired in a destructive, social-fabric-rending "race to the bottom."

In his book *The Great Disruption*, Francis Fukuyama demonstrates with an ocean of statistics how much healthier the United States—and to some extent, the leading Western European countries—has grown during the 1990s. Crime figures rose steeply everywhere in the western world (except Japan) from the 1960s until the early 1990s. Then the trend began to change. Other indicators of social dissolution—the abortion rate and the number of single mothers living on welfare—have also begun to fall.

"Something changed in about 1991 or 1992," Fukuyama told me. "American society has become more normal. We have full employment. People aren't living on welfare; they go to work in the mornings." Statistics do not, of course, provide exhaustive knowledge of a situation, and they can be manipulated. Has crime really diminished, or is it being reported less? But anecdotal evidence seems to confirm the beneficial trends.

"I grew up in New York," says Fukuyama. "People there are venturing out in the evenings again, going to theaters and restaurants. And here in Washington, D.C., I can see friends and acquaintances

moving into downtown areas, something they would never have done 10 years ago. Today there is far less pressure to move out into the suburbs. . . . The trends of the past few years are going to continue. It'll be more of the same."

Indeed, despite a few blips on the charts, the United States has improved its economic position throughout its history. In a report on "The Declining *Real* Cost of Living in America," prepared for the Dallas Federal Reserve, the authors point out that real cost of living has gone down over the decades, using as their gauge the amount of work they estimate regular workers require, on average, to purchase a particular good. By this measure, the cost of a half-gallon of milk has fallen

> from 39 minutes in 1919 to 16 minutes in 1950, 10 minutes in 1975 and 7 minutes in 1997. A pound of ground beef steadily declined from 30 minutes in 1919 to 23 minutes in 1950, 11 minutes in 1975 and 6 minutes in 1997. Paying for a dozen oranges required 1 hour 8 minutes of work in 1919. Now it takes less than 10 minutes, half what it did in 1950. The money price of a 3-pound fryer chicken rose from $1.23 in 1919 to $3.15 in 1997, but its cost in work time fell from 2 hours 37 minutes to just 14 minutes. A sample of a dozen food staples—a market basket broad enough to provide three squares a day—shows that what required 9.5 hours to buy in 1919 and 3.5 hours in 1950 now takes only 1.6 hours. . . .
>
> It's true that from 1970 to 1996 the work-time cost of a square foot of housing rose just over half an hour. [But] these days we're getting more home for our money. Today's new homes are more likely to come with central heat and air-conditioning, major kitchen appliances, a garage, an extra bathroom or two, ample insulation, storm windows and many other extras. The basic price of today's new homes includes these amenities, so it's impossible to calculate exactly what's happened to the real cost of housing. But it's a safe bet that the added features more than offset the extra 10 percent of work time. . . . Two-thirds of Americans now own their own home—the highest percentage in history and up from 45 percent in 1920.
>
> Much of what's in our homes is getting cheaper, too. Over just the past 27 years, consumers have benefited from work-time declines of 60 percent for dishwashers, 56 percent for vacuum cleaners, 40 percent for refrigerators and 39 percent for lawn mowers.

America's continued prosperity belies the view of the world presented by the critics of globalization. The irony is that John Gray's thesis of the Brazilianization of the United States was launched in

1990, just before America began recovering from the recent slump. Fukuyama insists that the "new economy," i.e., the information-based, Internet-driven economy, simply does not portend social collapse like that experienced by the United States from the mid-1960s. Although the causes of any country's bouts of domestic malaise will always be hotly debated, they're much more likely to be found in culture, ideology, and public policy than in the expanded economic opportunities afforded by international trade.

What's next? There are some good signs of late in the arena of public policy. But it is still an open question whether the trade policy of the United States will grow more optimistic and liberal, or more pessimistic and protectionist. In either case, the consequences will be global.

11. The Cult of Secrecy

Zejna Kasic is a Muslim refugee in her 50s who lives in a town not far from Sarajevo. She provides for herself and her family—an almost-blind husband and a mentally retarded daughter—by knitting pullovers.

The arbiters of international trade haven't made it easy for her.

On the occasion of the August 1999 Sarajevo summit, which attracted many of the world's leading politicians to a pompous celebration of stability and co-operation in the Balkans, the *Wall Street Journal* published a remarkable article about Zejna and others like her by Gregory Rushford, publisher of a bulletin on trade questions. Rushford had visited Bosnia's war-torn capital, where Zejna and more than 500 other Bosnian women refugees were taking part in a project sponsored by Norway and financier George Soros. The idea was to give the women a chance to earn an independent livelihood by making clothes, mats, and fabrics.

And it's a good idea. But until recently, such employment has been hobbled by the European Union. For years, pullover-knitters in Bosnia have not been allowed to export their products to the huge European market right next door without incurring an 11 percent import duty. They have also been banned from selling more than 2.5 million pullovers a year to EU citizens—a quota the Bosnians have shared with the Croats.

As Rushford observes, the situation is far from unique: "From the war-ravaged Balkans to the poorest parts of Asia, Africa, and Latin America, women like Mrs. Kasic are trying to sew their way out of poverty. That ought to mean every serious advocate of women's rights bringing pressure to bear to eliminate the cruel tariffs and quotas which the United States and Western Europe have instituted." When Rushford asked the retiring EU Commissioner for trade, Sir Leon Brittan, to comment, Brittan hid behind the Commission's press spokesperson in Washington, D.C., who declared textile products to be a "sensitive" matter.

Of course, Bosnia is one of the Balkan countries where Europeans and Americans have spent billions struggling to create peace and stability. And at the Sarajevo summit, many wise words were uttered about the importance of economic cooperation and free trade. But for the women of the region, a different reality has long applied—a reality of trade barriers and nebulous "sensitivities" of trade policy that add up to less food on the table.

* * *

If the elites have betrayed us, it's not because they worship Hayek but because they worship "security"—a security gained by foreclosing opportunities.

In Brazil the elite struggled to create security for a chosen few even as they created the utmost insecurity for the vast majority. But all systems of social security mean added burdens, added risks for somebody or other.

The price of protecting "sensitive" European textile manufactures is paid by refugees struggling to survive. The price of keeping China and Taiwan out of international trade policy forums—and postponing the market openings their inclusion would entail—is being paid not only by Americans but also by large numbers of Chinese. Those who pay the steepest price are typically outsiders with no ability to influence policy.

The cost of protectionism has been estimated at 7 percent of the EU's combined GDP—something like $600 billion a year. *Cui bono?* The immediate winners are the companies in protected industries, which reap bigger profits than they might have in a free market. Some ordinary people also win—people who otherwise might have become unemployed (at least temporarily) or had their wages cut (at least temporarily).

In 22 well-guarded sectors, however, EU policy "protects" no more than 200,000 European job opportunities, at a cost of $43 billion. This means that every thus-blessed worker imposes a cost of around $215,000 a year in protection money, enough to give every thus-coddled employee a new Rolls-Royce for Christmas—every year. The real cost of every job "saved" in this manner is in fact much higher, though; for if protectionism were to end, most of the 200,000 workers affected would soon find new jobs in more competitive industries.

In anti-dumping provisions target allegedly unfair competition from foreign companies. In reality, they are used to punish firms that engage in strategies that are routine—and legal—in the domestic market being protected. It would be a mistake to believe that anti-dumping duties are imposed only when an exporter sells goods overseas at a lower price than he does at home, the ostensible criterion of unfairness. In fact, home market prices are often ignored. Instead, the import police calculate "normal" prices based on arbitrary assumptions on costs of production, profit margins, etc.—none of which is a static or given factor and all of which can themselves be affected by anti-dumping regulations.

In anti-dumping laws, double standards proliferate. Consider the case of Sun Microsystems, a U.S. company that now gives away office software suites for free—trying to pull the rug out from under competitors like Microsoft, which charge hefty sums for such software. Could Sun's initiative run into trouble with the import police? Under GATT, there is a special agreement that aims to stop companies from selling stuff too cheaply. And there are government authorities charged with the task of ensuring that consumers need not suffer such unwanted generosity. According to laws in both the United States and the European Union—and a growing number of Asian nations, to boot—foreign companies that "dump" their goods are fair game for punitive tariffs.

But computer software seems to be exempted from the usual protectionist theology. When European customs officers determine duties on shipments of software, they include only the value of the storage medium—the floppy disk or the CD-ROM—in their calculations. So Sun's predatory giveaway will probably keep getting a free pass, at least for now.

Manufacturers of hardware are not so lucky. The EU has imposed anti-dumping duties on floppy disk manufacturers from, among others, seven Asian countries. One must forgive newly industrializing nations if they believe that global trade rules are rigged to favor rich countries at the expense of poor ones. That's how it looks when sophisticated software packages made in the United States and Western Europe may be dumped freely, while products for which countries such as Estonia, Egypt, Thailand, and Taiwan hold the competitive edge, from bed linens to fax machines, suffer punitive tariffs whenever they become too competitive for comfort.

Anti-dumping duties are considered an exception to the standard import duty. That does not mean, however, that the basic tariff structure is more equitable. In fact, the duties levied on imports from developing countries are on average 10 percent higher than duties levied on imports to developed nations. Import duties levied on products coming from the poorest of the poor countries (the so-called "least-developed countries," or LDCs) are 30 percent higher than the average. Anti-dumping regulations thus further skew a regulatory regime that is already biased against the poor.

* * *

European citizens may believe they're being generous when they demonstrate solidarity with European farmers, shoe manufacturers, chemical industries, and electronics and banana importers by giving up cheaper goods. But much of the bill is imposed on less affluent Chinese, Poles, Thais, Brazilians, Africans. The EU policy on agriculture is perhaps the most blatant example, second only to the policy (now at last revised) on Bosnian sweaters. The annual support that the OECD countries provide to agriculture ($350 billion) is worth twice as much as the agricultural exports from developing countries ($170 billion).

A large part of the price of the common agricultural policy (CAP) is of course paid by *insiders*—by European taxpayers and consumers. But a large share of the cost is also foisted onto outsiders—non-EU farmers who can't sell as much of their produce to Europe as they otherwise might have. According to the United Nations Development Program, developing countries are deprived some $60 billion of income thanks to the West's agricultural subsidies and high tariffs on textiles and clothing. It's a lose-lose situation, except that those in developing countries lose comparatively more, having less to begin with.

And it's a paradox. The economic core of the EU is the single market—an arrangement premised on the notion that free trade across national borders is a good thing after all. When Pascal Lamy was nominated to succeed Sir Leon Brittan as the EU's Trade Commissioner, the international press applauded the nomination as a politically deft move. After all, who better than a French socialist to convince France of the merits of free trade? But the real question is: Why should the EU need to be persuaded of the merits of *global* free trade at all, when the prospective trading partners are Asian rather than European? At least the Swedish left, relatively pro-free-trade as Europeans go, can see the injustice of the situation. In an article co-authored with Left Party members Lars Ohly and Marianne Samuelsson, Sweden's trade minister Leif Pagrotsky noted that while the EU is "comparatively open to the outside world. . .this does not apply in fields of particular importance to the developing countries, such as agriculture, textiles and clothing." So the EU must show greater openness and "solidarity" with the rest of the world by letting trade happen.

Nor is Western Europe's chronic mass unemployment—stimulated by labor market regulations that obstruct hiring—a cost borne only internally. In Europe, the social consequences of mass unemployment, how it marginalizes and segregates, are both visible and debated. More indirect, less visible, and less debated are the consequences for the rest of the world. Institutionalized unemployment strikes hard at the poorest people in the poorest countries. In 1999, the International Monetary Fund estimated that Europe's gross domestic product would rise by at least 4 percent if the unemployment rate were shrunk from 11 percent or so to 5 percent. In early 2001 European unemployment was still 8 percent or so. A boosted employment would raise the living standard of European citizens, in turn creating a bigger market for people in the less developed countries. The increased production would also help reduce or eliminate European deficits, thus releasing capital for the poorer countries, which stand to benefit more from cheap capital. And it could result in boosting European assistance to countries ravaged by war and natural disasters.

The use of anti-dumping regulations for protectionist purposes increased dramatically during the 1990s. When one duty was reduced or rescinded, two more were tacked on. Between 1990 and 1995, the number of anti-dumping cases reported to GATT/WTO increased by 1,000 percent. In 1999, 86 new anti-dumping investigations were initiated by the European Commission. A virtual explosion, considering that only 99 investigations were initiated in the preceding three-year period. By contrast, in 2000, there were only 31 new investigations—something of a return to normalcy, according to the EC.

Grumble as they may, Europeans can afford the astonishingly protectionist regime under which they live, the price for "solidarity" with their farming and textile industries. But what about the peoples of Latin America, Eastern Europe, and North Africa? And who is to pay the price of the social clauses and environmental clauses that so many advocate? If, as now, the decisions are made in Washington and Brussels, it's a fair bet that those who can afford only bicycles will subsidize the moral posturing of Rolls-Royce owners.

On this globe, 1.2 billion people live on less than a dollar a day. Freeing up trade is certainly not the only thing that must happen if they and other poor people are to be given a fair chance to escape hunger and material deprivation. But is there any other realm in which Europe and the United States can do so much for so many so easily, and with immediate payoffs for themselves as well?

The welter of protectionist arrangements in the West is above all *morally* questionable. It is unjust to stop innocent people from engaging in mutually beneficial exchange; it is unjust to stop them from escaping unnecessary poverty. If American presidents, European prime ministers, and others truly want to give a human face to the global economy, they should—right away—abolish all duties and quotas affecting trade with the world's poorest countries.

The main targets of the anti-dumping action have been producers in developing countries and in countries struggling to emerge from communism. For Bosnia and Zejna Kasic, at least, the trade wall is finally coming down. Humanitarian concerns about Bosnia and other former Yugoslavian regions clash too obviously with the visible harm done by protectionist barriers. So in November of 2000, EU ministers meeting in Brussels agreed to eliminate quotas on textile imports from Bosnia and Herzegovina, effective March 2001. These states must, in turn, liberalize duties on textile and clothing imports from Europe. But "sensitive" textile imports from Bosnia will still be watched like a hawk, to make sure nobody is sneaking in a sweater or pullover from some currently less favored country of origin.

Every once in a while a trade wall comes down. But how many Zejnas are there in how many other lands, suffering how much tragic waste of opportunity, because of the walls that are allowed to stand?

12. The Mental Wall

The place: Panmunjom, Korea. The time: early spring 1999.

The land seems peaceful, with neither people nor machines visible in the yellowing field of the valleys. The mountain tops are bare, like the trees; it will be a few more weeks before the willows bud. The only signs of life are the birds. Sparrows twitter, magpies organize their nests, and geese walk the dry paddy fields. Wild ducks traverse the sky over what Bill Clinton called "the world's most dangerous place."

There is a natural beauty about the miles-wide demilitarized zone that cleaves the Korean peninsula from coast to coast along the 38th parallel. The area is so inviting that conferences are held about how to preserve it when peace finally comes to the Korean peninsula. For a state of war still officially prevails. All that was accomplished in July of 1953 was a ceasefire. For now, the wild flora and fauna flourish within a sanctuary of barbed wire, mines, and opposing armies numbering more than one-and-a-half million men.

A visit to the zone is a poignant reminder that the Cold War is not quite over, not yet. That there are still frontiers which only birds, animals, and spies may cross—even in this age of globalization, this age without borders. Panmunjom is barely an hour's drive from Seoul, the capital of South Korea. It is the only place along the border where even a minimum of contact between North and South is permitted. There's a stately building there, ready to receive travelers, check mail, process goods through customs, and carry out all the routine tasks associated with border crossings. Except that there are no travelers, no mail, no goods. The appurtenances of cultural exchange taken for granted everywhere else in the world are inconceivable on the border between the two Koreas. Major General Sven Julin, who heads the Swedish delegation to the supervisory commission of the neutral countries, aptly calls Panmunjom "the capital of Absurdistan." He himself lives in an American military barracks, painted red with white corners—the style of a Swedish vacationer's countryside cottage—and dubbed Valhalla.

From a military observation post on a Panmunjom hillside you can look out over the Democratic People's Republic of Korea. There, on the other side of the military demarcation line marked by rusty yellow signs, is the socialist fatherland, exemplifying the Great Leader's ingenious theory of *juche*—national economic self-reliance and self-sufficiency. There you can see the world's tallest flagpole, 160 meters, from which, on this particular day, an enormous North Korean flag hangs lifeless. In the shade of the flagpole are uninhabited tower blocks. They are part of an entire Potemkin village created to impress the hapless denizens of the South, those impoverished serfs of neocolonial American and Japanese oppression who know nothing of Comrade Kim Il Sung's doctrine of liberation, nor of the heaven on earth he built just an hour's drive from Seoul and all its ugly and corrupt capitalism.

As late as the 1970s, it was uncertain which of the two Korean development models was superior, socialist dictatorship in the North or capitalist dictatorship in the South. In 1953, South Korea had a higher GNP per capita than the North. By 1970, the North had caught up and bypassed the South. North Korea seemed the more successful of the two countries. By 1975, South Korea had regained its lead and began to pull ahead. Today there can be no doubt: The average Korean in the South is at least 10 to 15 times richer and infinitely freer than his famine-prone relatives in the North. In 1993, the North had a per capita GNP of $904, while the South had a per capita GNP of $7,466.

If the South fell into the dreaded globalization trap, the North was snared by the isolation trap. But it has become clear that self-imposed isolation, not globalization, is the real danger to human society. The migrating birds over Panmunjom ignore the tightest and most heavily guarded border in the world to set their beaks firmly in the direction of the European spring and summer. Nature moves about freely; a human being trying to escape would be shot.

But the untrammeled communism and trammeled enclosure of North Korea are now the exception. Stalinist regimes elsewhere have fallen. Borders have been flung open.

At the end of the 1980s I visited the Great Wall of China, just north of Beijing. The barren, mountainous landscape was surmounted by the greatest barricade ever erected to protect against foreign threat. But mighty as the wall and its symbolism were, they could hardly compete with the sight of little old ladies in dark blue Mao costumes selling red-and-white cans of Coca-Cola to the tourists.

Ten years later I visited Berlin and saw 25,000 people on roller skates gliding along Unter den Linden and through the Brandenburg Gate, where for so long the Berlin Wall had divided East from West. By this demonstration, they were demanding that the traffic bylaws be amended so as to re-classify wheeled skates as "vehicles" rather than "toys." Apparently that would confer improved traffic status.

Coca-Cola and roller skates. Trivial, perhaps, but the kind of trivia that marks the transformation the Great Wall of China and the Iron Curtain into historical curiosities. Whereas the Great Wall is just a gigantic tourist attraction now, the Berlin Wall has been reduced to mementos: Fragments of it are on sale in the tourist shops, pasted to postcards and souvenirs. If this is trivialization, it's a trivialization that represents a giant step forward for human freedom.

In one respect Marx and Engels seem to have gotten it right. In the *Communist Manifesto* they observed that the bourgeoisie, "by the rapid improvement of all instruments of production, by the immensely facilitated means of communication, draws all, even the most barbarian, nations into civilization.

The cheap prices of its commodities are the heavy artillery with which it batters down all Chinese walls, with which it forces the barbarians' intensely obstinate hatred of foreigners to capitulate." Soft drinks and skates are more dangerous to economic and political dictatorship than all the soldiers of the world.

But it took far longer than Marx and Engels could have imagined for the walls to crumble. In China's case, the wall began to lose shape, figuratively speaking, only in 1979, when Deng Xiaoping gave his imprimatur to market reforms. In Berlin, the wall collapsed in a heap a decade later. Thanks to these two signal events, over the past 20 years more than two billion people have emerged from the isolation trap and entered the global market economy.

Much is new, but the old ways retain their power. In North Korea, Kim Il Sung is dead but kim-il-sung-ism lives on. But North Korea is not alone.

Has the mental wall come down, for example, in Brazil?

"No, it hasn't," said Rio de Janeiro entrepreneur Donald Stewart. "It's in the process of coming down—very, very slowly."

Germany?

"Definitely not!" snaps Mathias Döpfner, editor-in-chief of the daily newspaper *Die Welt*, in his office at Checkpoint Charlie. There's more mental masonry standing in Berlin than anywhere else. "We ought to build the wall up again—this time two feet higher!" say embittered Berliners. They are half-joking but also half-serious; the cost of unification has been high.

People want to tear down the walls and have them too. Everywhere the notion lives on that you can have both free trade and protectionism. Both free-flowing capital and political control of capital markets. That the welfare state can be reformed while leaving its infrastructure intact.

We want both the new and the old. West and East. Left and right. A Third Way.

13. Third Ways

"The 1990s began in Berlin and ended in Seattle," writes Moisés Naim, editor of *Foreign Policy*, in a turn-of-the-millennium editorial.

> In Berlin, a crowd tore down a wall built to contain democracy and free markets. In Seattle, another crowd rioted against the World Trade Organization in an effort to rebuild walls that might shield them from the ills unleashed by "globalization." Put another way, the bricks that people collected as souvenirs from the Berlin Wall in 1989, they tossed through the windows of McDonald's in 1999.
>
> Thus, a decade that began with great hopes about the global spread of capitalism ended with widespread apprehension about it. What happened?

Good question. Why *do* so many people want to build new walls to replace the ones that have finally come down? Is it because globalization has failed us?

Starting in the mid-1970s, the world started getting a lot more prosperous; global capitalism was the engine of that prosperity. The Asian "miracle" was the first stage of the process, and the pace of change was stunning. In South Korea in 1970, few people had refrigerators in their homes. Today everybody has one. And Korea, of course, was just one of a succession of Asian tigers. The whole region boomed until 1997. Then came the run on the banks, stock exchange collapse, currency crashes. Negative growth. Unemployment. The nouveau riche became nouveau poor.

Many have called the Asian crisis a crisis of globalization. True, insofar as the crisis did affect the "newly globalized" Asian middle class. Had they never gained any wealth to begin with, they would not have lost it. Also true, insofar as certain circles in Europe and the United States began raising new questions about globalization and liberalization of the world economy.

But not true in the sense many critics intend. The Asian crisis was not spawned by globalization per se. The responsibility lay at the feet of corrupt politicians and their bureaucratic cronies—and a sanguine middle class that wasn't paying enough attention to what the politicians were doing. At root, the Asian crisis was a series of domestic crises.

Indonesia is an illuminating example. Following that country's spectacular economic belly flop, the Indonesian capital of Jakarta filled television screens around the world. Demonstrations, riots, murders, rape, arson, lynchings, and looting in that country were suddenly daily headline fare.

Yet, when I visited Indonesia in the autumn of 1998, the debate on globalization was conspicuous by its absence. The Indonesian people clearly wanted a new *Indonesian* order—not a new international order. That was why President Suharto, who had ruled the country since 1966, was finally given the boot in May 1998. Hadi Soesastro, Head of Research at the Center for Strategic and International Studies, a Jakarta think tank, told me that Suharto got a lot of the blame for the country's troubles. "The crisis was caused by the corruption and nepotism of the regime. Our eyes haven't been opened to the problems of globalization."

Today Indonesia may seem to be a complete economic failure. But despite the recent turmoil, that's not so.

"Indonesia is still the country which has had the fastest social mobility in modern times," says the Sino-Indonesian historian Onghokham during lunch at one of the city's big hotels, owned by a son of Suharto. "Indonesia in 1950 was a lot worse off than it is today. At that time the country had only a couple of thousand educated people. The economy was dominated by a handful of Dutch conglomerates. In the past few decades, the bureaucracy, the army, police, and the economy have been very successfully Indonesified."

But despite the evident benefits of the market in even a troubled society like Indonesia's, many remain reluctant to embrace the market. The socialist model has collapsed, sort of. But that doesn't mean we're stuck with unbridled capitalism, does it? Might there not be a Third Way that allows us to escape from dichotomies?

Ulrich Beck has argued that the truly definitive mental wall of the postwar era was indeed "either/or" thinking. Since the toppling of the Berlin Wall, this binary prejudice has been supplanted by an all-embracing "and." Antitheses have dissolved. Ideology is dead. History has ended.

It is ironic that the "failure of globalization" in Indonesia and elsewhere is proffered as a rationale for a supposed new and improved political path, this Third Way that can navigate deftly between the Scylla of totalitarian control and the Charybdis of anarchic liberty. One of the more eccentric and tragic politicians of the postwar era was the first president of Indonesia, Sukarno, who affected to reconcile all social conflicts in his own person: "I have made myself the meeting point of all trends and ideologies. I have blended, blended, and blended them until they became the present Sukarno." But the economic devastation wrought under Sukarno looked a lot like what happens when old-fashioned one-way tyranny reigns.

Sukarno, brutal architect of the Third Way of Bandung and the Non-Aligned Movement in the 1950s and early 1960s, sounded a lot like the Social Democratic third-way thinkers of today who, like Beck, claim to be transcending the dichotomy of left and right. Thus Britain's Tony Blair—a politician who, with some success, has mixed, remixed, and then remixed the remix until evolving into the man he is today—feels comfortable declaring before the French National Assembly that there is "no economic policy of the left and an economic policy of the right, but only a good and a bad policy." What a relief. All we now have to do is choose between good and bad. And who wants bad?

The question, of course, is, What *is* good policy? And there isn't much unanimity about that—least of all among European social democrats. Marx-inspired traditionalists are still doing battle with Thatcher-inspired innovators for control of the agenda, acting very much as if they still believed in left and right.

In their joint manifesto calling for a modernization of European social democracy, *Europe—The Third Way/Die Neue Mitte*, Tony Blair and Gerhard Schröder wrote that today's voters want politicians "without ideological preconceptions. . .who, applying their values and principles, search for practical solutions to their problems through honest, well-constructed and pragmatic policies." Of course, few voters are likely to favor dishonest, badly constructed solutions to their problems. But this banal pronouncement does not succeed in explaining how a politician can remove his "ideological straitjacket" without simultaneously abandoning his values and principles, which are the sort of thing ideologies are made of. What *are* principles like social justice, solidarity, and liberty but seams in the ideological straitjacket? And it is raising a straw man to suppose that ideological commitment must imply blind, unthinking dogmatism.

At the end of the day, it is only in light of values and principles that political action can be defended. Unless a politician is willing to be a mere weather vane propelled by impulses of the moment, ideological guidance of some form or another seems unavoidable.

In the real world, knowing what is right and also doing it is a pretty tall order. But in the world of the new social democrats—at least in the world of their rhetoric—paternalistic politicians know it all and can do it all. They seem to believe that politics can transcend not only ideological dogmatism but also the realities of political economy—grasping politicians, hidebound civil servants, parasitical vested interests. But it is just as difficult for politicians to emancipate themselves from ideologies as it is for ideologies to emancipate themselves from vested interests.

And for all their avowed aversion to ideology, social democrats can still seem pretty ideological where the market is concerned. The war against capitalism is still high on the agenda of social democrats who claim to accept globalization. In his book *The Third Way*, Anthony Giddens, sociology professor and guru of the "new" social democracy, goes so far as to argue that regulation of money markets is the most important of all questions in the world economy. And many a European leader would agree that international capital must indeed be tamed. Balanced.

But it was precisely the attempts of the Asian governments to "balance" free markets and comprehensive governmental controls—with appropriate deference to such venerable Asian values as strong belief in authority and hierarchy and aversion to individualism—that caused the crises of 1997 to begin with. Market processes were hampered and distorted; corruption was given official protection; and economic problems were allowed to fester and accumulate. But far from acknowledging that the Asian situation points up the shortcomings of at least the Asian version of the third way, EU leaders join with the Asian leaders in regarding "the market" as their common enemy. On a visit to Singapore not long before he became prime minister in 1997, Tony Blair declared his profoundest admiration for the Singapore "model," characterized by free trade, a strong state, and communitarian values. Not much later, in April 1998, leaders of Asia and Europe met in London to ratify the notion that the Asia crisis had been induced primarily by a capricious market that had inexplicably lost confidence in the region. Another factor, they allowed, was the International Monetary Fund's lack of adequate resources to deal with the situation. But they did not acknowledge any policy failures on the part of the Asian governments themselves.

The ideological retreat of the left is of course welcome. But it is contradictory. And the contradictions pave the way to a policy which, practically speaking, brings little in the way of real change and progress. In the blend of opposites that the Third Way is said to represent, it is one side of the opposition in particular toward which third-way practitioners tend to lurch when push comes to shove. As old walls fall, new walls are hastily built to replace them.

Which makes the Third Way seem an awful lot like the old way.

14. The Future Is Open

Thomas L. Friedman compares globalization to the rising of the sun: "Generally speaking, I think it's a good thing that the sun comes up every morning," he allows. "It does more good than harm. But even if I didn't much care for the dawn there isn't much I could do about it. I didn't start globalization, I can't stop it . . . and I'm not going to waste time trying."

But perhaps developments are not quite so automatic as that. Maybe the sun will rise only if enough people really want it to be warm. (And realize that the burning orb in the sky has something to do with the heat.) Human beings built the Berlin wall and human beings tore it down. It will take a lot of political determination to demolish the walls that yet remain. The fact that the mercantilism and crony capitalism of the Asian states have managed to survive the systemic crises of the 1990s shows that what is economically "necessary" need not be even conceivable, politically. Europe, for its part, is still stymieing its own markets—for example, the labor market (through regulations) and currencies (through monetary unions)— and clearly intends to keep traveling down the same road. It's a road that leads only to low economic growth, high unemployment, and social polarization.

To the economist, protectionism may seem an irrational phenomenon, proof of economic illiteracy. But to politicians of all shades, the logic of mercantilism and protectionism is self-evident. It is in defense of European civilization that Thai rice, Chinese bicycles, and Bosnian pullovers are forced to bear heavy import duties.

To politicians, and certain of their constituents, walls confer a certain sense of control. That sense of control was always somewhat illusory, of course. All the walls in the world could not have saved the Eastern European communist dictatorships from collapse once the people had grown tired of living a lie. Economic walls in the form of trade restrictions and capital controls—erected by both sides during the Cold War—were also porous. People smuggled and bought and sold goods on the black market. Nevertheless, many people want that feeling of control. They want the state to "not row, but steer," as Blair and Schröder put it.

Reports of the death of the national state are greatly exaggerated. And as long as there are states, those states will likely always be reluctant to leave well enough alone. Free trade and free movements of capital are profoundly at odds with the nation-state. The Swedish economic historian Eli Heckscher has described how mercantilism emerged from the need of European Renaissance rulers to gather rival groups into more ordered political structures, which developed into what we today call "nations." Mercantilism, then, is the very wellspring of the nation-state. Economic protectionism also attended the founding of states outside Europe. America's own Founding Fathers were, many of them, overt protectionists. In several of the ethnically and religiously divided countries that came into being as a result of postwar decolonization, economic mercantilism has been perhaps all that holds the nation together.

British Prime Minister Tony Blair's concern with "Re-branding Britain" and "Cool Britannia" demonstrates the importance which even leading reformers of social democracy attach to the old national state. As political scientist professor Francis Fukuyama at George Mason University remarked, "No trade union or socialist party in the West can mobilize support for a program aimed at raising the standard of living in foreign countries; protectionism on a national basis is the only valid war cry." However globalized economies become, the social democrats and trade unions are unlikely ever to lose their national—and nationalist—character. Western trade unionists invariably consider American jobs and wages, or European jobs and wages, as the starting point of their arguments. What the West has been able to accomplish must already have been accomplished by other countries with whom we would trade, else we should not trade with them at all. If anything, globalization has only strengthened the political longing to bolster national-state communities, as those who feel themselves threatened close ranks to shut out the world. This reactionary nationalist phenomenon is, of course, itself global, with European social democrats playing only minor variations on the America First themes of Pat Buchanan.

And Marxist class thinking, discredited though it may be, still provides the ideological gloss for nationalist impulses. Classical Marxist ideals—and ancient distrust of capitalism—remain very influential in all the Western European social democratic parties and trade unions. Leftish critics of globalization blame it for the decline of the European "model," saying that low-wage competition from the developing countries, free movements of capital, and disloyal fiscal competition—coupled with a few internal "mistakes" like inefficient wage formation, bad monetary policy, clumsily handled deregulation of capital markets, etc.—are what has paved the way to economic stagnation, unemployment, and widening social gaps. But: "We can counter the power of global financial capital with the solidarity of the labor movement if we want to!" says Bertil Jonsson, chairman of the Swedish Trade Union Confederation. "And if we want to we can replace the class society with a society of solidarity, equality, and democratic socialism!"

But that is an old refrain, and Marxism has failed, as have its pale imitations. The planned economy doesn't work. Keynesianism doesn't work. Labor market regulations are counterproductive. But European, left-wing-inspired writers on the theme of globalization—Zygmunt Bauman, Ulrich Beck, Anthony Giddens, John Gray—nevertheless hope to "reinvent politics" by administering artificial respiration and cardiac massage to the corpse of Marxism. No third-wayer pins his hopes primarily on "the invisible hand"—what Hayek calls its spontaneous order—of the unhampered marketplace. (Not even John Gray, who wrote a book on Hayek.) Bauman thinks it is "folkloristic" to believe that economic liberty promotes wealth. He prefers the kind of storytelling that extol the virtues of walls.

The journalist Daniel Singer, in his book *Whose Millennium? Theirs or Ours?*, suggests that the Western European left will have to either create a radical alternative or give up. He himself wants to revive the utopian spirit of 1968. "We're not tied to the system," he writes, "and nobody can prevent us from looking beyond the capitalist horizon. We cannot just wash our hands and pretend. We are not doomed to impotence and inaction by fate."

Singer is right, at least, that the future is not ordained. Many people today seem to think that the "we" of classical liberalism—with the backing of globalization—has already won the ideological debate against socialism. There is perilous complacency among the traditional advocates of the market economy. Paradoxically, it may well be rooted in a Marxist view of history—the notion of certain economic and technological changes making the liberal, globalized market economy a historical necessity. The Internet is declared a "neo-liberal" technology. So the outcome is a foregone conclusion. There will be less nationalism and more globalism, less collectivism and more individualism, less state and more market. End of story. So why waste energy on the political and philosophical barricades?

But the future is going to be a lot more edge-of-the-seat than that. For all its rhetorical concessions to the market, European social democracy is not liberalism in disguise. The collapse of totalitarian communism has augured less well for liberal democracy and the market economy than many at first supposed. Marxism-Leninism may have failed, but it is just one of the many ideological enemies of the liberal market economy—ranging from the Romantic poets to the Roman Catholic Church and Persian ayatollahs. And that hostility to capitalism dies hard. Lately, talk of the Third Way is starting to wane, but the politicians ruling Europe at the beginning of the millennium still want to "create" jobs and "steer" capital. And they often govern with the parliamentary support of expressly anti-liberal parties.

In Germany, old-guard communists imported from the former East Germany maintain surprisingly strong electoral appeal, forcing more mainstream parties, including Schröder's half-modernized social democrats, to form coalitions with them at state and local levels. The Swedish government is characterized by parliamentary cooperation between the ruling Social Democratic Party and two anti-market parties, the Left Party and the Greens. The Left Party, according to the party program it adopted in 2000, is a "socialist" party which, on a "theoretical basis" of Marxism, is working for "the abolition of capitalism" and "democratic control of the economy." A couple of years later it was denigrating globalization as the progeny of "neo-liberal demands for the deregulation of trade and privatization in absurdum having been allowed to rule without restriction." These developments, the Left Party maintains, must be reversed. "The neo-liberal world economy" and its "international speculative markets" must be combated through "global taxes" and "democratic control of capital." According to Green Party spokesman leader Birger Schlaug, Western liberalism is comparable to Nazism and communism. For Schlaug, globalization is "free trade without responsibility," and it "claims victims every minute."

Clearly, the collapse of Marxism does not mean that collectivism and irrationalism have been uprooted once and for all. It is still much too soon for the advocates of capitalism and globalization to claim victory. Considerable progress has been made on the liberalization front in Europe during the past 20 years, often against the odds. But market advocates still have a lot of work to do. Core ideological conflicts will endure, whatever the latest labels. Nationalist sentiment will persist, as will the struggle between those who want to tear down walls and those who want to keep them up.

Tomorrow the sun will rise, yes. That much is certain.

15. French Fries vs. the Goddess of the Sea

Okay, so maybe the economic arguments arrayed against globalization aren't too persuasive.

But what if globalization is causing us to lose our very souls?

What if ever-expanding markets threaten to standardize and plasticize not merely this or that western redoubt of free enterprise, but the entire world? What if globalization is progressively smothering everything that is most distinctive and appealing in the world's cultures and replacing it with nothing but standard-issue widgets and strips of potato?

As globalization progresses, are cultures, countries, companies, and individuals being forced to adjust themselves willy-nilly to an American standard?

Writers often paint a picture of rival capitalisms. The main contenders are Europe, the United States, and Japan. Thus we have Japanese and European capitalism doing battle with the American variant, which, for the time being, has the upper hand. The first two are considered more "social" forms of capitalism, while America is said to represent a "cruder" version—as symbolized by the global hegemony of the McDonald's french fry.

British philosopher John Gray knows how the battle of the capitalisms will turn out: The worst will triumph, as ordained by what Gray calls "Gresham's new law." Gresham's original law says that bad money drives out good. The logic is simple: If two precious-metal coins of the same denomination differ in their pure-metal value—one is pure gold, say, and the other is half-gold, half-iron—then the coin with the higher metal value can be melted down and exchanged for the debased coin at a favorable rate. Finally, the good coins will be almost entirely withdrawn from circulation and only the debased coins will remain. Bad money drives out good.

Similarly, Gray argues, global laissez-faire can lead only to the better forms of capitalism being expelled by the worst form. Instead of metallic value, what's being diluted is the degree of "social responsibility" assumed by the alternative capitalisms. The high social cost of the "better" capitalist models of Europe and Japan puts them at a permanent disadvantage in a world of free trade and free movements of capital. Laissez-faire melts those models down. The worst kind of capitalism, in Gray's opinion, is (surprise) the American kind, which will therefore prevail. For the time being, anyway. In the long run, socially irresponsible American capitalism will be self-destructive, says Gray.

Of course, the assumption that America's capitalism is the "worst" capitalism available is more than a little dubious, given the prosperity and well-being U.S. markets have made possible. But in any case, Gresham's law is based on a state of affairs in which all factors but one (the value of the metal) are equal. It is hard to imagine any cultural and social factor except social spending ever being rendered identical in all the different countries of the world. If Gray were right, production and investments would be attracted to the countries with the least burdensome social systems. But Burma, where national government expenditure in 1997 totaled only 10 percent of GDP, is not the country to which all the world's industrialists and bankers are flocking. Clearly, then, their calculations must be influenced by something other than social welfare expenditure. But what? Political and social stability is one key consideration. Macroeconomic policy another. Economies are complex, as is their global interaction. A capitalist's prospects can be either enriched or debased by many different factors.

Gray's cartoon image of murderous competition between economic cultures is nonetheless a firmly established one. In the potato factories, defective potato strips are discarded if they do not conform to McDonald's measurements. Is global capitalism the equivalent of a totalitarian french fry factory? Or does it afford scope for local variation?

* * *

All happy families are alike, and so is every french fry. One strip of potato is much like another. The market insists on uniformity.

French fries are one constant on the McDonald's menu, everywhere in the world. Every other entrée can be adapted to cater to local tastes. In the Philippines you can order a McSpaghetti, in Thailand a pork burger with chili and basil, in India a Maharaja

MacMutton burger, in Japan a teriyaki burger, in Norway a salmon burger, in Uruguay an egg burger. The cola too is sweetened according to local preference.

But the french fry is standardized and immutable.

Of course, the variety of the rest of the McDonald's menu belies worries about an ever more culturally regimented global palate. But so does the global journey of the french fry itself. In a prize-winning series of articles for *The Oregonian,* business reporter Richard Read follows the global journey of the french fry from its beginnings in American soil to its final destination in the mouths of hungry Indonesians, and finds local color at every turn.

Unlike the fries, the producers and consumers who take part in the potato's global journey are astonishingly various. By the end of the story, the spuds have been "grown by members of a Germanic sect, sanctified by Moslems, transported by Protestants and consumed by Jews and Chinese converted to Catholicism in Asia. All of those along the french fry chain participated while retaining their beliefs and traditions."

The journey begins in a Hutterite colony, where 18 families farm 20,000 hectares outside Moses Lake in eastern Washington state. Like the Amish people, the Hutterites adhere to a strict religious tradition. Their men's dress also resembles that of the Amish: black trousers, suspenders, and hat.

The Hutterite variant of Christianity is rooted in 16th-century Germany and Switzerland. The name comes from the hatter and Anabaptist Jacob Hutter, who was burned at the stake in 1536. The life of the Hutterite colonies is dominated by their centuries-old traditions. There is a daily service. All property is held in common, common ownership being, according to the Hutterites, an expression of Christian love. The guiding principle is "to each according to his needs." The members do not have personal bank accounts. They differ from the Amish in at least one important respect, however: They use modern technology. They may not have televisions in their homes, but the members of this 400-year-old sect are all in favor of IT farms, infrared air photography, computerized harvesters. They exploit every conceivable technology to maximize production. Investments in computers and information systems have made it possible for them to analyze the impact of fertilization, irrigation, and spraying on every square foot of land.

And thanks to the worldwide popularity of America's fast food restaurants, including among the growing Asian middle class, the Hutterites have found a ready market for their potatoes. Since the mid-1980s, global demand for deep-frozen American french fries has escalated. Within the space of 10 years, export volumes have tripled. In Asia alone, sales doubled between 1993 and 1997.

The Hutterites sell their harvest to big American french fry manu-facturers like J. R. Simplot. To qualify for export to Moslem countries like Indonesia, foodstuffs must earn the coveted Halal stamp of approval (i.e., be certified as prepared in accordance with Moslem tenets). Upon arrival in Indonesia, the fried potato is served to the country's new middle class at McDonald's, Kentucky Fried Chicken, California Fried Chicken, A&W, Wendy's, and the rest.

Food plays a pivotal role in all cultures. The culture of food is bound up with identity and ruled by religious precepts and taboos. Tell me what you don't eat, and I will tell you who you are. Food is a powerful symbol—so powerful that globalization is sometimes dis-paraged as "McDonaldization."

The fear of McDonaldization is the fear of losing cultural identity. McDonald's is a symbol of the global spread of American values, hence a symbol of the threat which that global spread allegedly poses. Two arguments get trotted out here. The traditional one says that McDonald's, Burger King, KFC, and Taco Bell represent an American imperialism that is homogenizing the world's cultures. According to this view, McDonaldization will eliminate the cultural diversity which man has so arduously developed over the course of thousands of years. This is not too persuasive, especially to those who have taken the trouble of visiting a foreign land. All the cultural diversity is still there.

Lately a (slightly) more sophisticated argument has been making the rounds, instructing us that McDonaldization is okay so long as we remember who we are and keep in mind the cultural identity of the restaurant and its food. We do not lose our Chinese or Indonesian or Indian soul until we cease to recognize McDonald's as American. But then we do. The standard example features Asian children visit-ing America who, upon spying the golden arches, exclaim to their parents: "Look, they have McDonald's here as well!" These children are deemed to have lost their cultural compass—to have gone astray in the globalist jungle. (When they get home their parents will have a nice long talk with them, over a couple Maharaja MacMutton burgers.)

But such perspectives betray a superficial image of human culture and history.

* * *

Every March, Taiwan celebrates its Matsu festival, during which the Taiwanese address their prayers to Matsu, goddess of the sea. The temples are crowded with people and filled with burning incense and crackling fireworks. Eyes run and ears ring. Young and old, men and women—everyone comes. Wearing Mickey Mouse T-shirts and Reeboks and with mobile phones hanging at their belts, they present their votive offerings: fruit, cognac, eye shadow, and skin lotions. A goddess in the age of globalization shall want for nothing.

Matsu was born in 960 A.D., on the island of Meizhou in the Fujian province of China. She became a vegetarian and lived a life of innocence. By the time she was 16 it was clear that she possessed supernatural powers. In a dream she saw her father and two brothers drown after their fishing boat had capsized out at sea and rescued her father and one brother, but awoke before she could save the second brother. Later it became known that one of her brothers had indeed drowned at sea, but that her father and the other brother had miraculously survived.

Matsu died when she was only 28, but rumor of her powers spread far and wide. Chinese fishermen and sailors invoked her assistance whenever they found themselves in peril on the sea. In every port frequented by the Chinese, a temple was established in her honor.

It is easy to understand why sailors pray to a sailors' goddess. They are afraid. The sea on which they venture forth every day is both terrible and wonderful. It provides riches, and it claims lives. But what about modern, nonseafaring Taiwanese—what do they have to fear?

A lot. Taiwan is itself a cockleshell of a boat, on its own in a stormy sea. The communists on the mainland could capsize it any day. The fruits of the sea must be harvested while there is time. With Matsu's help, the Taiwanese have survived both political tempests and economic typhoons. They have a lot to be grateful for. Matsu deserves her cognac.

In Taipei, in March of 1999, I spoke with a leading expert on the Chinese ethnic cultures of Taiwan and Southeast Asia. Yih Yuan Li is a cultural anthropologist and a member of the prestigious Academia Sinica. I mentioned the debate on McDonaldization and cultural regimentation. "It's not true!" he replied, with an impatient shake of his head: "These are only superficial phenomena. The observable culture—the material culture—has been globalized, but the deeper cultural levels remain fundamentally traditional."

Yih explained that like any other culture, the Chinese culture can be regarded as two-tiered. The first level consists of everything visible to the human eye. The deeper level consists of that which we cannot see only with our eyes—what Yih called "cultural grammar": notions of man and of his relationship to nature and the supernatural, for instance. "Both Taiwanese and mainland Chinese," said Yih, "have retained their traditional concepts."

In Chinese culture, for example, a person can acquire supernatural powers. The concept is akin to the Catholic idea of sainthood—exemplary humans can be endowed by God with powers that can be invoked by the devout. But the Chinese do not believe in God; they believe in superman. There are no gods in traditional Chinese religion, only (super)men and women, like Matsu. (And the levitating warriors of the recent Academy-Award-winning film, *Crouching Tiger, Hidden Dragon*.)

"In the Chinese temples," Yih observed, "we worship 'ordinary' human beings."

The Chinese also have a distinctive view of "space." They imagine a particular space to be inhabited by destiny-shaping forces. To succeed in life, one must enlist these invisible forces—for example, by positioning one's home and office as favorably as possible. The doctrine of adjustment to these forces is called feng shui. Global transmission belts travel in both directions, of course. The Taiwanese have American french fries, and the Americans—and the rest of the world—have *Feng Shui for Dummies*, which "guides you through the fundamentals of the 4,500-year-old Chinese art, without bogging you down with technical jargon."

Visiting Taiwan we can see for ourselves that modern, urban Chinese eat hamburgers, drink Coca-Cola, talk on the phone, surf on the Web, sip red wine, and so on. Just like middle-class people everywhere. Global cultural "regimentation," in other words.

What we do not see so easily is that Chinese hamburger eaters have quite a different picture of the world. Take, for example, the way they look at food as medicine. Thus you eat specific ingredients because they are good for particular functions of the body. Cognac, in other words, is incorporated in a local, cultural grammar. The Taiwanese have not become Frenchmen.

Yih explains that the immense popularity of cognac in Taiwan 10 years ago was based on the belief that it is good for male potency. Now it is red wine that is becoming more and more popular in the Chinese cultural sphere, because it is believed to be generally good for health. "The Chinese drink alcohol because it's good for the body. Westerners drink because it's fun and enjoyable," says Yih.

We should beware, then, of jumping to conclusions about the relationship between material and spiritual culture. One does not merely imprint the other. A glass of red wine doesn't mean the same thing everywhere. Nor does a hamburger. Not even the standardized french fries have a standardized cultural content. The goods may be global, but their meaning is always local. So the Chinese do not cease to be Chinese the moment they get their teeth into an American hamburger. To do that, they would have to assimilate a foreign cultural grammar that simultaneously displaces their own.

That day is likely to be a long time coming—in any country. There are as many cultural grammars as there are languages. Cultural diversity is not threatened by global commercialism.

No one need sell his soul for a french fry.

16. The Freedom Gap

Freedom is not good for Asians. It's not their way, Asian leaders tell us.

During the late 1980s and early 1990s, whether "Asian values" could be compatible with liberal democracy was the subject of some-times heated international debate. Many writers argued that since Asians place such a high premium on order, harmony, collective welfare, authority, and the like, western-style democracy was un-suitable for them.

According to Singapore's Lee Kuan Yew, in the United States the "expansion of the right of the individual to behave or misbehave as he pleases has come at the expense of orderly society. In the East the main object is to have a well-ordered society so that everybody can have maximum enjoyment of his freedom. This freedom can only exist in an ordered state and not in a natural state of contention and anarchy." In 1993, ministers and representatives of Asian states gath-ered in Bangkok signed a declaration which stipulated that while human rights may well be "universal in nature," it is crucial to bear in mind mitigating "national and regional peculiarities."

Asian officials worry that by fostering individualism, democracy will breed chaos and conflict, eroding faith in authorities—which, according to the authorities, would be bad. Sure, in certain cases compromise might be possible and a rigged election or two might be held, so long as society and (more importantly) the authorities do not suffer. But you certainly can't have freedom of the press or, heaven forbid, "contention."

But at the risk of being contentious, let us ask: Why *can't* a social institution like the free press be incorporated by the existing cultural grammar of Asia just as the hamburger has been? If it is true that Asians are inherently averse to individualism, that aversion would be reflected in the region's democratic institutions. The press would not be as confrontational and critical of authority as it is in the West, for instance. But of course, the fear is that at least some Asians will like individualistic freedoms just fine, and would have no problem being critical of authority. Indeed, there would be little need to fear democracy if submission to authority were as culturally inevitable as it's often made out to be.

Since the Asian economic crisis—which highlighted the dangers of fixed-exchange-rate regimes and crony capitalism—the strident triumphalism of Asian values has faded. But the debate over the relationship between social and economic development and cultural values continues. Just before Christmas of 1998, I had lunch with the Malaysian author and consultant Foong Wai Fong in Kuala Lumpur and asked her if the West still has something to learn from Asia. She replied that the "Asian virtues"—hard work and avoiding dependence on the state—are still of great relevance. No doubt that's so, even if one could argue that these values are more universal than Asian.

In any case, such virtues have not been enough. And perhaps they have also become vices. The emphasis on self-reliance may have lapsed into a kind of amoral retreat into the family, a situation in which the typical response to government incompetence and misrule is a shrug of the shoulders. Foong says that political awareness and participation must be established as core Asian virtues as well.

But that will take a lot of doing.

"The Western mode of political systems must never be copied!" China's President Jiang Zemin has proclaimed. With one exception, of course: the political system of communism itself. "We must cherish the socialist regime built upon the blood and sacrifices of countless martyrs. We absolutely cannot carry out the West's model of bourgeois democracy; for if we do, chaos in China is inevitable." It is a tragic irony that communism—a quintessentially European ideology with roots stretching back to Plato—manifests itself in the new millennium as a predominantly Asian phenomenon. Indeed, Marxism-Leninism is practiced hardly anywhere now but China, North Korea, Vietnam, and Laos.

Although for some years so-called Asian values were lauded for promoting prosperity, it is now often said that it was a culture of corruption, nepotism, and collusion that paved the way for the region's recent economic crisis. In this respect, the debate has returned to an older pattern, in which Asian underdevelopment was attributed to the region's "culture." Decades ago, the economist Ludwig von Mises argued that the reason Asia has often fared worse than the

West in modern times is that the East "lacked the primordial thing, the idea of freedom from the state. The East never raised the banner of freedom, it never tried to stress the rights of the individual against the power of the rulers."

Many modern champions of Oriental despotism—from Lee Kuan Yew in Singapore and Mahathir Mohamad in Malaysia, to Suharto in Indonesia and Hun Sen in Cambodia, to Jiang Zemin in China and Kim Il Sung in North Korea—have insisted that freedom is not the Holy Grail Western liberals say it is. According to today's Asian philosopher kings and sultans, it is national order that matters most. "Freedom" is just a perfidious Western notion that foreigners try to deploy, like some Malaysian pig virus, in order to destabilize local regimes.

But is it really true that Asia lacks indigenous libertarian traditions?

Clearly, neither the Chinese nor the Indian classical tradition of government has provided much ammunition for individual freedom-seekers. But while China has known many periods of repression and xenophobia, it has also known times of greater openness and liberality. Tom Palmer, a senior fellow with the Cato Institute, reminds us that the southern Sung dynasty of the 12th century was characterized by rule of law, advanced financial institutions, low taxes, and free trade and openness—in contrast to the Yuan, Ming, and Ching dynasties that followed. Editor and translator Brian E. McKnight notes that during "the remarkable period of more than two centuries from the late T'ang into the Southern Sung, China developed a thoroughly monetized economy, with the invention and spread of the use of paper money, the widespread use of a variety of other paper instruments for commerce, an enormous increase in minted coinage and the use of other mediums of exchange, including precious metals and silk. . . . The luxury trade of earlier times gave way to a thriving trade in daily necessities." And on the cultural side of things: "The tensions between Confucian social commitment and concern for the self was complicated by a new emphasis on the importance of self-discovery and the self-improvement of the individual." So the story is far from being one of uniform repression and love of order.

The scholar Anthony Reid identifies a more recent but still largely forgotten tradition of liberty indigenous to Asia in southern

Sulawesi. There, in what is today Indonesia, the Bugis people established a liberal political order in the 18th century. In the Bugis state of Wajo, based around Lake Tempe, seafaring entrepreneurs developed a political outlook centered on the concept of *merdeka*, freedom. Historical chronicles and other documents from the area detail "the freedoms of Wajo." Reid argues that there was a clear connection between the individual entrepreneurship of the Bugis people and their attachment to an "ideology of freedom." Regrettably, the liberal Bugis tradition made little impact on the political culture which came to dominate Indonesia.

* * *

"So where was the first conference held? Pyongyang?"

That was the response I got from the webmaster of FreeMalaysia.com when I asked what he made of the fact that Kuala Lumpur was slated to play host to "Global Knowledge II," the second international conference on the information revolution and developing countries. The event, held in March 2000, was sponsored by the World Bank and supported by a host of international development organizations as well as companies like Cisco Systems, Sun Microsystems, Dell, and Nortel Networks.

"Given the ruthlessness and comprehensiveness of the government's suppression of all other forms of free expression, there is no reason to believe that it truly wishes to promote wide access to a major conduit of independent commentary, such as the Internet," said the Malaysian webmaster, who prefers not to be identified.

For the record: The first conference was held in 1997, in Toronto. But it is true enough that Malaysia's mass media are increasingly being enlisted to create a Kim-Il-Sung-like cult of personality around Dr. Mahathir Mohamad, the country's prime minister. In 1999, Malaysian state television launched a 16-episode drama, "The Unfinished Struggle," based on Dr. Mahathir's life. A multimedia CD-ROM entitled "Mahathir, CEO Malaysia Inc." further caters to the curious. Those who really want to penetrate the doctor's mind might attend seminars on "The Thoughts of Dr. Mahathir." Meanwhile, the Malaysian media take care to reverentially record the prime minister's every pronouncement.

Malaysians who decline to glorify their "great leader"—notably, publishers of *reformasi* (political reform) Web sites—definitely feel the pressure from on high. The Malaysian ruling party's anti-defamation committee singles out Web sites that allegedly contain slanderous and defamatory statements about the government. These sites "jeopardize national security," according to the committee's chairman. FreeMalaysia.com is tagged as one of the most dangerous sites. Perhaps just by coincidence, the site's home page offers a prominent link to a "rogue's gallery" of Malaysia's politicians, at which may be found sharp criticism of "Dr. M.'s" concept of Malaysia Inc.—a notion of private-public cooperation that has, in practice, been "riddled with inefficiency and corruption well before the Asian financial crisis struck," according to the site.

"Rumors persist in the community of *reformasi* webmasters that a private security consultancy has been hired to track down these sites' operators—and that the government intends to act after this information is collected. Of course, this is a pretty paranoid group talking," noted one webmaster in an e-mail.

Paranoia? Well, sometimes they really are out to get you. In April 2001, a crackdown of *reformasi* activists—recalling the 1987 roundup of dissidents known as *Operasi Lallang* (Operation Wild Grass)—seemed to remove any doubt about the government's intentions. Today, though, the Malaysian authorities may find that the job of cracking down has gotten a lot harder: Dissent is more widespread, and there is more internal whistle-blowing about what the government is doing. The monitoring comes from both the government's own Human Rights Commission of Malaysia *(Suhakam)*, established in April of 2000, and from the Internet itself. While only 10 percent of Malaysians have access to the Internet, what gets published on the Web can be quickly printed out and disseminated by word of mouth. It will be hard for the government to put the genie back in the bottle—much as it might like to.

It may seem ironic that a government as free-press-shy as Malaysia's would host a conference on how to prosper from the information revolution. But Malaysia is hardly unique in that respect. Politicians and technocrats all over the world typically approach the challenges of the knowledge-based, information-driven economy as if it were just a matter of hardware, of technology and financial resources, and ignore the "software" questions of political attitudes and institutions. Today, many recognize the positive power of information to shape the future of individuals, communities, and nations.

But few understand the nature of the bottleneck that, especially in Asia, is stopping that potential from being actualized.

Two recent publications highlight the analytical tendency: the World Bank's *World Development Report 1998/99: Knowledge for Development* and the OECD's *Science, Technology and Industry Scoreboard 1999: Benchmarking the Knowledge-based Economies*. Both reports present readers with a wealth of statistics and trends: on digitalization of telephone systems, the proliferation of Internet servers, expenditure on research and development, mathematics test scores, national human resource profiles, etc. In all these areas, a "digital divide" is growing, we're warned. But neither report attends to such issues as freedom of expression and freedom of the press.

A free (and professional) press is one of the key institutions that enable individuals and countries to take advantage of the opportunities presented by the global economy—and to avoid its pitfalls. Yet Freedom House finds that only 69 of 186 countries it surveys enjoy a fully free press. The situation is particularly bleak in the Middle East, Africa, and Asia. In the latter region, only 6 of 24 countries boast a free press, according to the group's "Press Freedom Survey 2000." (Malaysia earns the lowest possible ranking—"not free"—along with countries like Chad, Kyrgyzstan, and Qatar.) This widespread "analog divide" (lack of access to an un-gagged media) is probably far more injurious to the development of poor nations than any "digital divide."

The case of Malaysia illustrates a commonplace technocratic bias. Ostensibly to meet the demands of the Information Age, the Malaysian government invests heavily in "hard" infrastructure. High-profile boondoggles like the Multimedia Super Corridor and Cyberjaya—attempts to cobble together a Silicon Valley out of the equivalent of old oil palm plantations—are prime examples of Dr. Mahathir's ambition in this regard. At the same time, Malaysian authorities busily manipulate and manacle the flow of information. It is this "Malaysian model" mingling of hi-tech sophistication with reactionary nationalism, IT with intolerance, that was showcased at the Global Knowledge conference. Other developing and newly industrializing countries are encouraged to follow the same path. The cult of hardware may make leading technology companies happy. But it rejects the rationale for the hardware—the free and open conveyance of information.

The importance of a free press in promoting economic growth *and* equity can hardly be overstated. According to Jean Michel Severino, vice president for East Asia and the Pacific at the World Bank, one of the most important lessons of the debilitating Asian economic crisis was "the power of information to support equitable growth and, conversely, the power of censorship or misinformation to distort it." The reason is straightforward:

> Investment decisions are based on information, and the quicker and more reliable the information, the less likely it is that decisions will be made on emotion and herd instinct. A free press, informed and well trained in the skills of analysis and investigation, may be one of the best resources a country can have in managing the challenges and taking advantage of the opportunities presented by the globalized economy. . . . The East Asian crisis has raised press freedom as a legitimate part of the development agenda, and there is every reason to hope and to expect that this critical issue will receive more attention and more support throughout the developing world.

Nonetheless, the executives at the World Bank—and at other international aid and development agencies—claim they do not have the authority to demand press freedom in the developing countries to which they lend money and give aid. But why not? After all, the fundamental principle governing the World Bank is the notion that it should finance projects for "productive purposes." And lenders and donors are more likely to mistakenly invest in wasteful projects in countries in which free flow of information has been choked off. The ability to deal with political corruption or environmental destruction is also hampered when there is little reporting on such problems.

So the World Bank and other aid donors have good reason, at least with respect of their own fiscal responsibilities, to pay more than lip service to the importance of free flows of information in recipient countries. Countries that lack freedom of the press should receive fewer and smaller loans from the aid organizations. And, because risks are higher, they should pay higher rates of interest than countries that do have a free press. (Of course, countries that do respect freedom of speech probably don't need much in the way of loan handouts, since they can likely attract private capital to finance development efforts anyway.) So far, the concentration of development financing to countries that gag their media has worked to entrench the status quo. Of the five countries receiving the largest net income from multilateral aid organizations like the World Bank and the International Monetary Fund, not one enjoys a free press.

No country can expect to develop a knowledge-based and information-driven economy unless its people are free to trade information and opinions. Bridging the gap between the haves and the have-nots, the knows and the know-nots, of the global economy requires not only access to new technologies, but also access to political freedom. So long as 80 percent of the world's population is denied access to a free press by their governments, the "information revolution" can only sputter.

* * *

Our perspective on the past shapes our visions—and our actions. If Asia is to truly embrace individual liberty, collectivist and statist culture must be recognized for what it is—as much a dead end for the East as it has been for the West.

Several years have now passed since the outbreak of Asia's economic crisis. Many people do realize that the region's problems have deeper causes than flaws in any "financial architecture," whether local or international. Yet, in capitals around the region, there persists a surprising degree of cultural self-righteousness and resistance to change.

Asia can achieve a renaissance. Whether it will, and how quickly, depends on how many individuals in Asia today—in the boardrooms and on the farms, in the halls of power and in the halls of academe—truly wish to see freedom, individualism, and creativity animate the soul of their societies. The first step is to recognize that freedom is not good merely for this people or that people, for Easterners or Westerners.

Freedom is good for everybody.

17. Watch the Grass Grow

But a country needs more than freedom to be successful in the global age. Community is also important.

Maybe one of the things Asia needs more of is sports.

As a European who lived for many years in Thailand, I found that one of the most distinctive features of everyday life there and in other Southeast Asian countries is the lack of enthusiasm for team sports. In Europe, as the role of traditional religious communities diminished, the rise of sports at least partly compensated. In the new industrial towns, football, rugby, ice hockey, and other team sports provide the population in general and male industrial workers in particular with a sense of identity and belonging. Football has become the new "opiate of the masses." But in Thailand and Malaysia, football fans typically care more about Liverpool and Manchester United than the local teams. Sports has a very marginal role in Asian societies. And Asia is the poorer for it.

Religious life may not have waned in Asia as much as it has in Europe, but the rapid transformation of society has noticeably diminished the sense of community. As Asia has industrialized and urbanized, traditional communities centered on temples, mosques, and village-based cooperative agricultural endeavors (like planting and harvesting rice, and the operation of village credit associations) have either disappeared or declined. Why has sports never fired the collective imagination of industrializing Southeast Asia? The fact that many of the modern-sector laborers are female may have something to do with it. Perhaps, also, the fact that many workers are seasonal migrants whose social roots and identity remain in the village. And while inhabitants of the gleaming cityscapes remain well-off in economic terms, even after the economic contraction of the late '90s, they remain relatively poor in terms of social capital. It is not entirely surprising, given the fact that large cities hardly existed in Southeast Asia a generation or two ago.

According to political scientist Robert Putnam, social capital consists in "features of social organization, such as trust, norms, and networks, that can improve the efficiency of society by facilitating coordinated actions." Building social capital requires people to relate to each other beyond the confines of immediate personal concerns and interests. It also means fostering values like greater openness to outside influences, receptiveness to democracy, and friendliness toward commerce. Without strong communities, it is hard to see how democratization and political decentralization—laudable trends— can provide good government and meet the expectations of citizens over the long haul. When individuals and families focus only on their own problems—as remains the case throughout much of Southeast Asia—problems endemic to the whole society are left unresolved. Without "trust and ties" at every level of society, it's hard for businesses to plan for the future.

Some argue that social capital doesn't matter, when it comes to economic development. The tentative conclusion of economist John F. Helliwell's study of Asian societies is that variations in the degree of economic openness may be sufficient to explain all differences in economic growth in Asia. Helliwell finds no positive links between social capital and economic growth. Other observers tell a different story. Robert Putnam's influential study on Italian democracy argues that patterns of civic life explain why some regions of Italy have prospered while others remain mired in poverty and corruption.

Economist Grace Goodell argues that the attempt to economically jump-start a society without first laying proper social and cultural foundations—as they were laid in England and the United States prior to their industrial and political revolutions, for example—must ultimately backfire. "In India and many other nations, the entire country participates in formal, macro-level elections with formal political parties, while virtually no decentralized field of interaction in the whole society can claim predictability, from the poorest village to the circles of industrial giants. Without local predictability, how can there be rational allocation or bonding? Indeed, despite the trappings of democratic participation, most Third World societies have far less leverage against centralized arbitrariness at every level than did European peasants of the Middle Ages." There has not been enough social development "on the ground" to permit truly robust and consistent development at the macro level in such societies, argues Goodell.

To be sure, some kinds of carefully and locally accumulated "social capital" may in fact inhibit economic growth. The caste system in India is one such example, limiting, as it has, the economic functions people may engage in. In some societies a raw decline in social capital of the wrong kind might prove beneficial from a purely economic point of view. But for the sake of a society's long-term health, one must hope that more positive beliefs and values emerge to replace destructive older ones.

Perhaps it requires a punch to the jaw for the economic consequences of social ills to be recognized. Social capital may not have mattered—not as obviously, anyway—during the "miracle phase" of Asian economic development. But as top-down, state-led development models reach the end of the road, Asia is learning that it must find a healthier path to growth. Some nations adapt faster and more effectively than others. Dani Rodrik concludes that societies that have weak institutions for conflict management suffer the hardest economic setbacks when they experience an external shock. If he's right, it is bad news that the countries of Southeast Asia are still woefully lacking in robust social institutions, strong local communities.

Analysts at IMF and the World Bank often argue that crisis-hit Asian nations need to introduce "good governance" into their societies. But the phrase is vague and vaguely understood. Good for whom and for what? Left unspoken is the fact that "good governance" often means "good for capitalist development." And that "good governance" is brought about by good politics and good culture. But how can these be achieved? By whom? And where to start? "Like alchemists, Western and Third World planners and rulers have focused attention on the surface—the economic, the aggregate, and the statistically measured—before confirming the political and social foundations, the local, the regional, and institutional structures," observes Goodell. "In their singular drive to attain the former, they have debilitated the latter, which are the underpinnings for sustained development."

Economists Rafael La Porta, Florencio Lopez-de-Silanes, Andrei Shleifer, and Robert Vishny find that standards of governance are worst in countries that are politically unfree, close to the equator, ethno-linguistically heterogeneous, use socialist or French systems of law, or whose populations contain large numbers of Catholic or

Muslim groups. These findings would seem to bode ill for Asia in general and Southeast Asia in particular. Japan excepted, the region's democracies are young and immature. Several countries—including China, Vietnam, and the other nations of Indochina—support a socialist infrastructure designed mainly to protect the ruling regime. Thailand, Indonesia, and the Philippines have been inspired in large part by Napoleon. In Indonesia and Malaysia, Muslims make up the majority of the population. In the Philippines, Catholics dominate. As far as ethnic and linguistic diversity goes, Southeast Asia resembles the Balkans.

The legal systems of Hong Kong, Malaysia, and Singapore have their roots in British common law tradition—the tradition that the researchers found to be most supportive of market-based development. In Hong Kong, however, it remains unclear whether the ex-colony's British heritage can survive being merged with the socialist legal system of the motherland; so far it is doing okay. And in both Malaysia and Singapore the legal systems have been so twisted by the powers that be that they have acquired a suspiciously French patina: The main function of the law is to protect the interests of the state and the party, not those of private citizens. Again, it seems clear that a lot of work has to be done "on the ground" to sustain even well-borrowed social systems.

Japan, South Korea, and Taiwan seem to have the best institutional fundamentals by these criteria: ethnically homogeneous populations, few Catholics or Muslims, and legal systems inspired by the German tradition, which provide a good base for capitalist economic development.

The ethnic and religious makeup of nations cannot be altered without great suffering and hardship, but two of the variables identified by La Porta et al. can be influenced by Asia's politicians—and its people. It *is* possible to increase political openness and strengthen democracy. And it is possible for legal systems to better protect citizens against meddlesome governments. During the past three decades, the Asian "tigers" have performed economic miracles. Now they have to become political and legal lions. Economic wonders that cling to authoritarianism and statism risk becoming economic also-rans.

Under the Asian social contract, citizens are expected to refrain from interfering with political governance so long as politicians and bureaucrats deliver fast economic growth and rising prosperity. That kind of civic forfeiture isn't tenable over the long haul. Asian citizens must learn to bother about questions beyond the immediate household. They don't have to become rugby or football fans to nourish their communities and reinforce the civil society, but they must find ways to form political parties and other organizations to express dissent and create change. They can, at least, object when they witness bad policies and their destructive consequences.

Some countries—Thailand, Taiwan, South Korea, and Indonesia, for example—have made impressive headway. But much remains to be done. Reupholstering a social system is not a quick and easy job; the attempt to make it so tends to backfire. In Indonesia's case, events are proving that overturning Suharto's *Ordre Baru* (New Order) was a piece of cake compared to erecting a workable replacement. It is easier to displace than to build.

Who will do the building?

"Keep an eye on the grassroots," Foong urges.

It is there—among engaged, ordinary people—that a new and progressive Asia is slowly taking shape.

18. Changing Crony Capitalism

Kim Joo Young is a young lawyer with his own practice. His office, in the heart of Seoul's financial district, is surrounded by skyscrapers bearing the names of the well-known Korean corporations. Bare gray branches sway outside the window; just across the street is the Seoul Stock Exchange building.

"Companies aren't a Korean invention," says Kim. "Shares aren't a Korean invention. They are foreign concepts that have been introduced here. But if we accept these aspects of modern capitalism, we also have to introduce the system of accountability that goes with them: shareholders' rights. That's the global way."

Kim wants Korean capitalism to grow up. "The history of capitalism in Korea is very short," he observes. He is a leading member of one of South Korea's most successful nongovernmental organizations, the People's Solidarity for Participatory Democracy (PSPD). In recent years the PSPD has attracted thousands of new members.

The Seoul Stock Exchange first opened its doors in 1956, but concepts like the accountability of company management to shareholders and respect for the interests of minority shareholders were not widely countenanced for another 42 years. That such concerns finally have come to the fore is largely thanks to Kim and the other PSPD activists. And, of course, thanks to globalization.

In 1997, the South Korean economy went down in flames when international banks and investors withdrew their money from the Korean peninsula. The Koreans—whose country had only recently been accepted into the Organization for Economic Cooperation and Development—were hard hit by the economic crisis. Unemployment rose sharply. So did the suicide rate.

The government that laid the foundations of the whole wretched business, headed by President Kim Young Sam, had adopted globalization—*segyehwa*—as its political lodestar. The administration had argued that South Korean society would have to be opened up and thoroughly reformed if it were to keep pace with the world's leading economies. But execution of that policy was ragged and inconsistent. Prior to 1997, South Korean politicians and vested interests were picking and choosing among those aspects of globalization that they liked (such as lending from foreign banks), while avoiding those aspects they found more burdensome but which would have promoted greater economic discipline (like foreign ownership of local companies).

After all the globalist rhetoric that preceded the crash, you might suppose that the drubbing the South Korean economy received at the hands of the global economy in 1997 would engender a strong anti-globalist backlash. There are, to be sure, not many friends of globalization among academic or trade-union circles; there, globaphobia prevails. But *segyehwa* is far from being politically discredited in South Korea, and globalization remains a force to reckon with. The country's current president, Kim Dae Jung, continues untiringly to preach the globalist gospel.

Like its neighbor to the north, South Korea has traditionally been afflicted with one of the most closed economies in Asia. Foreign influence in the form of investments, consumer goods, and culture had long been frowned upon. Since 1997, though, the regulators have started to relax a bit. In July 1999, South Korea's border was thrown open to imports of consumer goods and popular culture from neighboring Japan.

When the financial crisis hit South Korea, you could hear the mental walls beginning to crumble. Far from an indictment of globalization, the trauma was widely seen as a vote of no confidence in the South Korean model, dominated by gigantic, rapacious conglomerates called *chaebol*. And there were plenty of scoundrels to point to. One of them, Kim Woo-Choong, now enshrined in the *Guinness Book of World Records* as "the greatest manipulator of accounting books of the century," ended up fleeing the country after the pervasive book-cooking of his Daewoo empire was exposed. After the economic crisis hit, the Daewoo Electronics founder developed a nasty habit of faking assets and hiding debts—debts which added up to almost 50 trillion won by the time Kim Woo-Choong skipped town. Much of the money he borrowed ostensibly for investment purposes was in fact funneled into his own personal—and secret— British bank accounts. The rigged financial structures of South Korea helped make the massive deception possible. In the end, some 34

Daewoo executives and accountants were indicted for accounting fraud. But Kim Woo-Choong is still in hiding.

If Korea is now introducing reforms, it is not because of threats from such gunboats of western capitalism as the IMF. Change is being propelled by the desires of Kim Joo Young and other ordinary Koreans for greater openness and global norms. A former legal adviser to the *chaebol*, Kim has now switched sides. "I got tired of seeing how they were systematically breaking all the laws and regulations. Even if they are public companies, they don't care about shareholders and they ignore stock market law," he says. When the South Korean economy crashed in the autumn and winter of 1997, Kim joined many of his countrymen in blaming the collapse on *chaebol* mismanagement. He resigned from his job with one of Seoul's leading legal practices, set up shop on his own, and joined the PSPD.

Today Kim is a moving spirit of one of South Korea's most influential political movements, the campaign for the rights of minority shareholders. His goal: Clean up Korean business life. In Seoul, "shareholder value" is not a dirty word but a radical, progressive idea, a logical extension of South Korean democratization. Like the struggle for political democracy itself, the campaign for shareholder value represents a demand for social justice.

To achieve its ends, the PSPD cooperates with other minority shareholders, foreign ones included. The organization wants to change how South Korean corporations are managed so that they attend to the shareholders' interests as well as those of their founders.

The PSPD wants firms to comply, for example, with rules and statutes about information and decision-making. Until now, the "board meetings" of the country's leading corporations have been little more than a sham, with resolutions made in advance according to the top executive's own guidelines, and rubber-stamped in advance for the board members. Management holds onto the rubber stamps, which are used in lieu of signatures. The fiction of board meetings is sustained, but members needn't bother to attend: There's no business to discuss, no decisions to make. Nor would board members be likely to raise much of a ruckus in any case. They're all recruited internally. A seat on the board is like a gold watch, a reward for long and faithful service.

The PSPD also wants the banks to conduct a proper credit analysis before advancing new loans—instead of being guided by political pressure and the bribes of borrowers.

And it wants to put an end to the abusive practice of turning profitable *chaebol* units into cash-cows for new loss-making projects. Samsung Electronics, for example—a giant cash-cow—helped Samsung Automobile to get started by means of big loans and car purchases. The two firms belong to the same *chaebol*, but their shares are listed separately on the stock exchange. The transactions are not commercially based and, therefore, are detrimental to the owners of shares in the electronics company and unfairly beneficial to the shareholders of the car company.

In a succession of widely publicized cases, the PSPD took company directors and presidents of banks and *chaebol* to court. In July 1998, a court ordered members of the board of directors of Korea First Bank to pay the bank 40 billion won (roughly $26 million) as compensation for losses incurred through their mismanagement. "That was a one hundred percent victory for us; it was sensational," says Kim.

The victory encouraged the PSPD to inaugurate similar proceedings against other giants. The sins against minority shareholders committed by Samsung, Daewoo, and Hyundai are next in line to be reviewed by the courts. "If we can stop the subsidies from cash-cows, all the other *chaebol* companies will have to alter their way of doing things." Firms would then be obliged to resort to the open capital market for financing.

Openness of this kind would lead to greater corporate transparency and a more disciplined market. But it would also cause trouble for the country's biggest private corporations—and employers. The combined sales of the 30 biggest conglomerates add up to nearly 90 percent of South Korea's GDP. These powerful vested interests oppose the proposed changes. They claim that the market economy is a threat to South Korea's corporate culture, and would make it harder for corporations to compete in the world market.

But Kim makes the commonsense point that a country with well-run companies will flourish as a country with chronically inefficient companies will not. There is no inherent clash between shareholder value on the one hand and general prosperity or welfare on the other. On the contrary. During the 1990s the South Korean *chaebol* were allowed to indulge in a massive destruction of capital, eroding the economic resources of an entire nation.

Major reform is possible. And there is precedent. During the 1950s South Korea introduced land reforms. In 1944, the wealthiest three percent of farming households had owned 64 percent of all agricultural land. Twelve years later, the wealthiest six percent of farming households owned only 18 percent of the land. *Yang-ban*, the landed aristocracy, had lost its privileges. The land reforms opened the way to industrialization and to South Korea's economic resurgence. Equally sweeping reforms are needed today if the country's economy is to be emancipated from the new *chaebol* aristocracy.

Vigilant shareholders and other outside market agents are the only ones who can discipline company directors suffering from delusions of grandeur.

"The biggest corporations have a lot of power and influence over politics and the banks. Neither politicians nor banks can force the necessary changes. Only the shareholders can," says Kim. Junior managers in the mismanaged Korean companies are also getting involved. They know the problems firsthand, and many are discreetly tendering their personal support—in the form of financial contributions—to the PSPD's campaign against the financial abuses of their own employers.

For some time, foreign investors have been irritated by the mismanagement of South Korea's leading corporations, but they never dared to do anything about it, fearing a nationalistic reaction against foreign investment. But now, with local allies like Kim, they are able to put more pressure on *chaebol*.

"The PSPD has made a superb contribution and are getting a great deal of support from foreign investors," says Seok Yun, head of research at Credit Suisse First Boston in Seoul. The five biggest *chaebol* definitely feel threatened.

Small firms, which long resented the privileged and dominant position of the large corporations in the country's capital market, are also pleased with the changes that are under way.

"The civic movement for shareholders' rights is good for Korea. It spurs management to run their companies more efficiently and fairly. That in turn makes Korean enterprise more competitive," says Lee Hyo-Cha, head of the Korea Federation of Small Business. The *Korea Herald* also ratifies the effort, observing that by uniting global trends and local activism, civil organizations have emerged as "a leading force for democracy and change in every sector of society."

The activists are working to break up old economic structures which are more socialist than capitalist. Journalist Michael Breen, who has been reporting from Seoul for many years, wrote in his book *The Koreans* that while, on the surface, South Korea may have looked like a capitalist country, its customs and attitudes made it far more socialist in essence. Like the socialist regimes, South Korea has been more focused on production than on quality or profitability, and it has had a strange attachment to heavy industry (steel, shipbuilding, etc.). It also made use of planning and state-directed allocation of capital to create national "champions," the *chaebol*.

Although the system is not socialist per se—ownership remaining private—it is no coincidence that Asian communist governments seeking to reform their economies are enamored of the Korean model. China and Vietnam, too, want *chaebol*-like conglomerates to inhabit the commanding heights of the economy.

Prior to the crisis, Korea's big businesses were being subsidized by the state and by domestic banks at an alarming rate. In 1985, the five largest *chaebol* firms accounted for 16 percent of the assets in the South Korean manufacturing sector. By 1997, they held a staggering 40 percent of the assets. At the same time as cheap bank loans were being channeled into the Korean behemoths at unprecedented rates, their average rate of return on assets fell sharply. Consequently, as their share of output, employment, and exports ballooned, these companies became not only "too big to fail" but a financial disaster waiting to happen.

In the wake of the Asian crisis, a number of western observers attributed the wrecked regional economy to unrestrained global market forces. Kim begs to differ: The market forces were too weak, and still are, he believes. Market forces can do their job only if no firms are deemed too big to fail. Which is why law and justice are needed to spur the changes.

It's easy to say no one has to buy shares they don't like. Instead of suing badly run companies, why not just sell the shares and forget about them? In the long run, after all, market forces should be able to ensure that well-run companies are rewarded while those that disappoint are punished. Basically Kim agrees, but he says that, even so, it is not a viable strategy. The market is hampered not only by government intervention, but also by the inherited crony-capitalist structure of the market itself. If it had not been so easy for Daewoo executives to exploit sloppy or rigged financial structures, they might not have gotten away with as much fraud as they did.

The big Korean corporations are like black holes into which the savings of average Koreans disappear, never to be seen again. So it's not enough to sit back and wait for the market to deal with the problems. Every kick in the pants helps.

"Through the courts, we are hastening a process which has to come about anyway. But we won't go on forever. Gradually, responsibility will be transferred to the real shareholders."

Some action has indeed been taken to stem the worst excesses. Early in 2001, the government agreed to expand a rule that requires boards of directors to approve any transfers to subsidiaries worth more than 10 billion won and to disclose these to the public; the 30 largest *chaebol* are now subject to this requirement, which had hitherto been imposed on only the top 10 *chaebol*. The government is also preparing to introduce laws that would strengthen the hand of corporate boards and allow the minority shareholders to pool their votes.

Kim hopes it won't be too long before market mechanisms become sufficiently robust to make his work in the PSPD unnecessary.

19. A Course in Corruption

I met Sumalee Limpa-Ovart over a cup of coffee in one of the more remarkable districts of Bangkok, an area dominated by large, impressive buildings in Grecian style. On one side of the street, the façades conceal "massage parlors"—high-class brothels. Those on the other side of the street belong to the Ministry of Justice and the Supreme Law Courts.

Sumalee is a prosecutor, but has become better known in Thailand as a mother. An angry one.

Her daughter had been turned down by one of the finest schools in Bangkok, the Kasetsart University Demonstration School, which aspires to be an educational laboratory for elementary school teaching. Teaching standards and resources at Kasetsart are far above the norm. It's a very tough school to get into.

Nathanit was one of 2,500 seven-year-olds to take the entrance exam. Only 120—less than 5 percent—were accepted. That's not what angered Sumalee. That Nathanit was not one of the lucky ones came as no surprise to either mother or daughter, and Nathanit soon found a spot at another good school.

It was at this other school—which, unlike Kasetsart, openly published its exam results—that Sumalee found reason to suspect that there was something fishy about the admission procedure at Kasetsart. She recognized the names of children—their surnames those of wealthy or politically connected families—who had been accepted at Kasetsart yet scored poorly on the exam for her daughter's school. Sumalee visited the Kasetsart School and asked to look at the test results.

Nothing doing. Secret.

But she didn't leave it at that.

Just a few months before, the Thai parliament had adopted a new, more democratic constitution and the country's first public domain laws. Politicians and civil servants had long opposed democratization and the openness promised by the new laws. But the newly impoverished middle class believed that the crash of 1997 had been caused by an administration whose corrupt doings were being shielded from public view. They were fed up. They would no longer tolerate politicians and bureaucrats treating their offices as private fiefdoms. They demanded—and got—the right to information.

"Ever since law school I have thought that Thailand ought to have public domain legislation. Now we have it. And I decided to see if it would work," says Sumalee. It didn't. The school told her they had not heard of any principle of public domain. And so a legal war ensued that has lasted for years, ending finally in unambiguous victory for Sumalee. Her case was the first to reach Thailand's newly established Official Information Board. Higher authorities would become involved as well—including the Constitutional Council and the government.

It turns out that of the 120 students accepted in the year Nathanit applied, 38 scored less than the minimum requirement. These were not near misses. One successful applicant managed to chalk up only 15 points in the entrance test; the passing grade was 63. Nathanit had scored 68. How did Kasetsart's administrators account for these remarkable conditions? They pleaded that the parents of the 38 children "had been of special service to the nation." When journalists asked for more detailed descriptions of these special services, they received a familiar answer. Secret!

But it's not so secret. "Being of service to the nation" is a euphemism for gifts of money to the school, says Vipaj Vijitvatakarn, editor of *Business Day*. The admissions system of the national elite school has been based not on meritocracy but on aristocracy and plutocracy. In the end, the school was obliged to admit what it was doing. The names of the privileged children—names of rich and powerful families—were openly published, making clear that "contacts" and money are what have mattered most, not aptitude. Eventually, Kasetsart University president Theera Sutabutr would admit that Kasetsart did solicit and receive contributions from the parents of the privileged whose children were admitted to the school. Nobody had really supposed otherwise. But intuiting the truth is one thing; reading about it in the papers is another.

"The school's admissions system is discriminatory on economic and social grounds, which is prohibited by the constitution," says Sumalee. "In Thailand there is a group of students who get ahead through their own patient efforts. And there is a group who don't need to exert themselves because they can use their contacts. What sort of people will they grow up to be?"

In the old, closed society of Thailand, perhaps contacts and nepotism could work reasonably well. But not in today's global economy. Sumalee is anxious for school to convey the right values to children, teaching them that it is hard work and individual achievement that count.

"I want to prepare my daughter for globalization. She must be able to compete not only with other Thais but also people from all over the world," Sumalee explains. "I hope to set a precedent which can help lead to a gradual improvement of the situation in Thailand. Transparency and accountability will increase. Civil servants will find themselves in the spotlight. The worst that can happen is for nothing to happen, for nothing to get better. In that case, all the pain I and my family have suffered would be in vain."

Sumalee's struggle did ultimately prove successful. In early 2000, Thailand's State Council ruled that Kasetsart University Demonstration School's admissions policies were discriminatory and violated the country's constitution. The school was ordered to stop awarding preferential treatment to "privileged children." All state schools in Thailand must now comply with the ruling. (Many are complying, although Kasetsart University itself is now planning a new demonstration school that will openly retain a quota system. They argue that because the school will rely only on private funds, the quotas are not unconstitutional.) Legal mandates won't transform Thai society in one fell swoop. But many observers agree that Sumalee's case marks a milestone in the battle against nepotism and cronyism in Thailand.

Reformers elsewhere are following suit. Fifty-five-year-old Aruna Roy of India, leader of the right-to-information movement in that country, is one example. Despite the obstinacy of what she calls "status quoist" bureaucrats, her efforts have led to implementation of a right to information in Tamil Nadu, Goa, Rajasthan, and Karnataka—a modest beginning, but a beginning. "The right to information will lead to less corruption," Roy says.

* * *

Stories like those of Kim and Sumalee illustrate an often-overlooked reality in the debate on globalization: the opportunity provided by crisis.

115

In the late 90s, countries like Indonesia, Thailand, and South Korea were plunged into profound economic difficulties, including swelling unemployment. The suffering we can see instantly, and it cannot be shrugged off. But the crises also opened the way to progress, as citizens became more motivated to grapple with their society's shortcomings.

Thanks to the Asian crises, men and women like Kim and Sumalee have a chance to effect change. They are not prosperous young traders; they are not coupon clippers. They are not even idealogues. Just parents who want their children to grow up in a better, more just society than the one that they grew up in. And they know that globalization is a strong force on their side, a force that can help topple the walls that have sheltered corruption.

That's why the Asian crisis did not prove to be the comeuppance for globalization many critics had hoped for. Asians realized that the crisis had been produced by homegrown shortcomings, not any defects of "global laissez-faire capitalism," nor gaps in the "international financial architecture," nor any other such abstractions characterizing villainy from afar. South Koreans and Thais were up to their eyebrows in corruption, domestic corruption. Rotten banking systems. Rotten education systems. Rot too deep and widespread to ignore. In this context, the impetus of globalization came as a breath of fresh air.

The worst thing that can happen is for nothing to happen. But things *are* happening. In countries like South Korea, Thailand, and Indonesia, economies have been somewhat liberalized. Many old monopolies and oligopolies have been swept away. Democracy has made substantial progress. The watchdog role of the media has been strengthened. It is true that, four years after the outbreak of crisis, some reformers feel disappointed and frustrated. Despite passage of the Official Information Act in 1997, Thai officials are still loath to part with any information, and the Official Information Board has become mired in politics and red tape. A beginning has been made, but the will to implement new reforms seems to have faded. Change is not coming as rapidly as the Sumalees and Kims had hoped.

But it's coming.

20. Making It Happen

The place: a six-story block in Taipei. The name: Iwill. The motto: Make it happen.

Here, 145 hollow-eyed young people are making their dreams come true. They work long hours, often not returning home until two or three in the morning—if they go home at all. The people of Iwill have caught gold fever.

On the fourth story, a Siemens machine assembles 800 electronic components on a circuit board every 53 seconds. The manufacturing almost takes care of itself: Only one operator is needed to keep an eye on the machine, and half the production is farmed out to subcontractors.

The core of Iwill's operation is its development department, where 20 computer engineers work day and night to design the various computer boards—motherboards, SCSI adapters, sound cards, graphics accelerators—that speed up data transfer and thus enhance performance. These are the guys who put the turbo in the computer. They do it not by inventing new components, but by smartly combining and recombining components that already exist. Iwill is all about architecture.

Iwill products are in demand among computer users with unusually high speed requirements: advertising producers, designers, and other professionals who work with large graphic files. In the dawn of the computer age, customers mostly worried about whether the casing was labeled Apple or IBM. Now the cognoscenti are more interested in what the casing conceals, and the innards designed by Iwill top the charts in PC magazines all over the world.

"Now the customers are asking whose motherboard is in the PC. They know it's Iwill they want," says Mason Su, an Iwill founder and its managing director.

Competitors are breathing down their necks, and they know it. So far things have gone well. Iwill is one of Taiwan's fastest-growing companies. Between 1994 and 1998, sales increased almost tenfold.

"Every day there is just one thought in my head: Who's going to take my business away from me? I'm very paranoid," he says. He is also eager to keep staff happy. "The employees are my boss. Like me, they have shares in the company. They expect to be rich. If I don't live up to their expectations, make sure that their dreams come true, they'll walk out on me." As long as they stick around they'll at least be able to eat: Lunch costs a symbolic few cents in the company's well-appointed basement restaurant. And because so many people work late, dinner is also served—free of charge.

The keys to survival are speed and creativity, the ability to zap new ideas to the market. The product cycle is six months, max. Nothing can be taken for granted.

"Other companies can easily copy our products as soon as they are released," notes Mason, who is as energetic and intense in casual conversation as he is in business. "But by then they're already too late. They don't have time to organize the production and build distribution channels before it becomes obsolete and we've replaced it with a new version."

Iwill is one of Taiwan's largest and fastest-growing industrial enterprises. In 1997 it ranked 800th among Taiwan's biggest industrial concerns. Mason wants it to climb to 200th place. In the reception area hangs a photograph of Mason Su and President Lee Teng-hui of the Republic of China, taken when Iwill was nominated one of Taiwan's best "small and medium enterprises" (SMEs) in 1998.

Long workdays mean he doesn't see all that much of his wife and two children. An empty golf bag stands in his office.

"I don't play golf. It was thrown in when I bought a Lexus," he explains.

The PC revolution is a gold rush, for Iwill and for all of Taiwan. The Taiwanese churn out computers and accessories faster and cheaper than almost anyone else. Sixty percent of all motherboards are made by Iwill and its Taiwanese rivals. Taiwanese firms also account for 48 percent of the world's modem production, and a third of all notebook computers. Taiwan is the world's third biggest maker of IT commodities, right after the United States and Japan and ahead of Germany.

During the California gold rush, prospectors staked their claims, dug, panned. If they were lucky they struck gold and struck it rich. If they were unlucky, all they got was gravel. When luck—and gold—eventually ran out, there was nothing for it but to try all over again: Stake a new claim and start from scratch. Today's IT entrepreneurs follow the same path, except that their Klondike knows no boundaries. One can pan for IT gold in Taiwan just as well as in Silicon Valley. The fast, free flow of ideas, capital, and goods means that anyone—anywhere—has a chance to strike it rich. All it takes is a phone jack. And the supply of gold is endless.

They say it took almost a millennium for the wheelbarrow—a Chinese invention—to reach Europe. And another Chinese invention, the screw, took 1,400 years to make it to the west. Technology spread slowly, once. Not these days. Abetted by the ease of exchanging information on the Web, Iwill can keep instantly abreast of technical progress on the other side of the globe. The firm cooperates with the leaders of the PC industry like Intel and Microsoft, and belongs to the many global organizations in which the industry's technology trends are defined.

* * *

The PC systems now pervading our homes and workplaces are packed with gadgetry from firms based on the island which Portuguese seafarers 400 years ago knew as Ilha Formosa—"the beautiful island."

"Beautiful" is perhaps not the first adjective that comes to mind as you speed along the Sun Yat-sen Freeway from Taipei to Hsinchu, Taiwan's IT center. Though small, the island has a population of 22 million. And it shows. What the Taiwanese call "countryside" is simply densely populated industrial areas, small emerald-green paddy fields are randomly dotted with factories.

Taiwan is one of the world's more successful refugee camps. The first big surge of refugees from the mainland came in the 17th century, when Taiwan was governed by the Dutch East India Company and by Dutch Protestant missionaries. When the Ming dynasty fell to the invading Manchus, adherents of the old regime took refuge in Taiwan. The second big wave came in 1949, after the Communists defeated the Nationalists in the Chinese civil war. The Nationalist leader, Chiang Kai-shek, fled to Taiwan with a million of his followers. Mao Zedong, leader of the Communists, hoped to "liberate" Taiwan and ordered the People's Liberation Army to bombard the rebels. But the Communist invasion failed to materialize.

When Mason Su was born in 1958, Taiwan was under martial law and Generalissimo Chiang Kai-shek was still nursing grandiose plans for reconquering the mainland. In those days agricultural produce made up 90 percent of the island's exports. The Taiwanese were as poor as the people of Zaire and Congo. But 1958 was also the year Taiwan began liberalizing its economic policy. No longer protected from foreign competition, Taiwanese entrepreneurs would now be obliged to seek their fortunes outside Ilha Formosa. The process of liberalization has been slow; 40 years later, it is still incomplete. But gradually, Taiwanese entrepreneurs have been turned loose on the world market.

Small firms became the engine of the Taiwanese economy. Between 1961 and 1971 the number of SMEs more than tripled. Small firms grew faster still. They began by exporting textiles, shoes, and other simple, inexpensive products. Now they're shipping far more advanced articles, even as the old industries have migrated to the Chinese mainland and Southeast Asia to take advantage of cheaper labor costs. Over the last four decades, entrepreneurs like Mason Su have turned Taiwan into the world's fifth largest trading nation and its 18th biggest economy. The islander's average income has risen from the Congolese level of less than $200 a year to something like $13,000 a year, which means that the Taiwanese are better off economically than the EU citizens of Portugal and Greece, in spite of the massive EU assistance doled out to the latter.

The Republic of China was Asia's first democracy, by the 1950s already affording considerable scope to local politics. Beginning in 1951, provincial assemblies, mayors, and district councils were chosen in general elections. Opposition parties were banned, but "independent" candidates could stand for election and even defeat the candidate of the Kuomintang. At the national level, it took a while before democracy was allowed to function freely. But finally, in 1986, the "independent" politicians founded the country's first opposition party, the Democratic Progressive Party (DPP). Martial law was lifted in 1987. The first free parliamentary elections were held three years later. A presidential election was held in March of 1996—the first time ever that a Chinese head of state had come to power through the ballot box.

Only one step remained: a shift in power. That took place in March 2000, when the Kuomintang, which until then had enjoyed a decades-long, continuous monopoly on power, was defeated in the presidential election by the DPP candidate, Chen Shui-bian.

As democracy advanced, Ilha Formosa grew more attractive. In earlier decades, Taiwanese had gone to the United States for their education, and decided to stay there. But with the end of martial law, many Taiwanese expatriates decided to come back—including Mason Su, who had studied computer science at El Paso, Texas, between 1983 and 1989.

Asked what the state can do to make things easier for small firms, Mason Su gives a short answer: "What we need is more engineers and marketers. And free trade. There mustn't be any obstacles."

* * *

Computer nerds from high-tech countries are not the only ones who have a chance to strike gold in the globalized economy. Almost anyone can. From almost anywhere in the world.

In his book about the new Africa, *Into the House of the Ancestors*, journalist Karl Maier tells the story of Seni Williams, a globalized software manufacturer in Lagos, Nigeria.

Until recently, Lagos has had almost no viable infrastructure. If firms wanted electricity and water, they had to run their own power generators, dig their own wells (sort of like modern-day California). The economy had been run into the ground. Lagos would seem to be the world's most unsuitable setting for a modern IT entrepreneur.

But even here, opportunity beckons. The volatile economic and political environment has made it profitable for Williams and his firm, Tara, to develop an extremely flexible computer program, Auto-Bank, marketed to customers in the Nigerian banking industry. In Nigeria you never know what idiocies the central bank is going to think up next. Everything's in flux. So the banks must also be able to manipulate their databases' silly putty.

Deregulation and globalization have also revved the pace of change in American and European banks. Flexibility is in demand. Williams speaks of "the Nigerian factor"—a chameleon-like adaptability. "That's part of the Nigerian national character. But now it's become a global requirement." Which is why not only Nigerians do business with him. Oracle, a U.S. company that is a world leader in database software, has invested in Tara and is using the company's products.

After years of dictatorship, Nigeria's new democratic government is hoping to lure back some of the 15 million or so Nigerians who now live abroad. They're even phoning Nigerians living overseas and asking them to give their homeland another try. Along with the promise of political freedom comes the promise of electricity— efforts are under way to rebuild the country's sputtering power network.

So maybe Nigeria is getting a little less chaotic. But no matter how stable things get, one suspects that Seni Williams will always be able to find a market for his software.

* * *

Not even literacy is an absolute requirement for the global economy.

A few years ago I traveled up the Rejang River in the Malaysian province of Sarawak. On a tributary deep in the jungle, there is a longhouse, Rumah Atong—a sort of tribal apartment building that is home to an entire village. The tribe was once sustained by jungle logging operations. When the logging jobs disappeared, the Iban had to choose between moving into the towns or reverting to more traditional jungle living. They opted for the latter.

The Iban men help make ends meet by going off into the forest, to collect edible items and to hunt. But the women have taken a different path. They weave for the world market. Not just any old market: the discerning art markets of Paris, London, and New York. They are plugged into one of the most sophisticated realms of the world economy, but they don't even have telephone or radio links with the outside world. All communications go by boat, up and down the river.

And it works.

The Iban are perhaps better known as headhunters. In the days when the men were harvesting heads, the Iban women were on "the women's warpath," weaving ritual fabrics known as *pua*. Traditionally, *pua* were used in ceremonies associated with birth, harvest, death, and head-hunting. In the intricate patterns one can make out jungle flora and fauna, people, spirits. Every weave tells a story, a story first told in a dream. No Iban woman would dare weave a pattern without having first witnessed it in a dream; that would be taboo.

While the men have given up headhunting, the textile traditions of the women live on. A few years ago Edric Ong, a Malaysian architect with an interest in fabrics, came to Rumah Atong and asked whether the women might like to weave silk instead of cotton. Bangie Anak Embol, the head man's daughter, agreed to give it a try. Today the 50 weavers of Rumah Atong are internationally acknowledged textile artists, with prizes from UNECO, the World Crafts Council, and other bodies to prove it. Bangie and her colleagues go on world tours—to Gothenburg, London, Australia, Japan—to exhibit their wares.

The integration of Rumah Atong's weavers with the world economy has given their endangered craft, and the endangered culture of the Iban, a new lease of life. Not without tension. Gender roles have been turned upside down now that the balance of economic power has shifted emphatically in favor of the women. And the superior artistry of some is a cause for envy by others. But considering the alternatives, a little social tension is something the Iban village of Rumah Atong can live with.

* * *

This is how economic vitality happens, anywhere in the world. By the testing of ideas and the weaving of dreams. The gold-panners working themselves half to death at Iwill could easily have fetched nine-to-five jobs with a bigger company. But that wasn't their dream. Seni Williams could have stayed in the United States and worked for a Boston consulting firm. But that wasn't *his* dream: He wanted to return to Africa and do something on his own. The families of Rumah Atong could have drifted to the towns and become assimilated. Instead, they've made their mark by paying attention to *their* dreams, making them real, then sharing the fabric of them with the rest of us.

21. "We Are All Globalizers Now"

It is the last year of the millennium. The United Nations Conference on Trade and Development (UNCTAD) is convening in Bangkok. During the opening ceremony, a classical Thai dance troupe performs a dance based on the ancient Indian epic of Ramayana.

Phra Ram does battle with Thotsakan, king of the ogres, who has abducted Phra Ram's wife, Nang Sida. She is a reincarnation of Lakshmi, the goddess of prosperity. The drama unfolds in a slow and highly stylized fashion to the sound of haunting flutes and ominous drums.

This ancient tussle over the divine power to create prosperity is witnessed by several hundred politicians and diplomats, hailing from every corner of the world. They have more in common with the masked dancers on stage than they imagine.

* * *

I bring the minister bad news. The morning's search on the Internet for news on Bhutan had resulted in a single headline: *Kuwait 20, Bhutan 0.*

Khandu Wangchuk makes a face. It turns out that he is not only the minister for trade and industry of the government in Thimpu, the capital of this minuscule Himalayan nation. He's also president of the national soccer team.

The Associated Press reports that 20 to 0 is "perhaps the largest rout ever in national-team play," a dubious honor. When the minister returns to Thimpu, he will be greeted with taunts and jeers.

After centuries of self-imposed isolation, inglorious defeat is perhaps the inevitable price of Bhutan's entry into the world. But it is a price Khandu Wangchuk thinks his country should be willing to pay.

"People always ask me: 'How can you disgrace our country so?' I always tell them that it is through such disgraces that we will improve. If we don't play, we can't improve. We need the exposure," argues the minister, a man whose compact build reminds me of a boxer rather than a football player.

He has two major ambitions for his country. He wants Bhutan to gain membership in the Fédération Internationale de Football. And he wants it to be accepted into the World Trade Organization. To that end he attended the infamous WTO summit in Seattle, and then the tenth United Nations Conference on Trade and Development in Bangkok, in February 2000.

"If we don't join the mainstream we will continue to be marginalized," says Khandu Wangchuk. "Anything that depends on protectionism will have a hard time surviving in this day and age. We must promote our entrepreneurs. The destinies of nations are intertwined now. We cannot forget the rest of the world, and just be on our own. Of course, all countries have concerns about globalization. But we must find solutions together. It doesn't mean that you shy away."

Bhutan is definitely coming out of its shell. On June 2, 1999, the silver jubilee of King Jigme Singye Wangchuk's coronation, Bhutan formally launched its national television channel. Bhutan once had a ban on TV; it has been lifted. At the same time, Druknet, the country's first Internet service provider, came on line; *Kuensel*, Bhutan's only newspaper, can now be read on the Web. In October the government filed its application to join the World Trade Organization. And it is preparing a policy and legal framework to encourage foreign investment. All this 11th hour effort to join the world community marks a watershed in the history of this extremely conservative mountain kingdom. As recently as the 1960s Bhutan had neither roads nor any kind of telecommunications.

The controversies and sometimes violent confrontations surrounding the WTO have not dampened Bhutan's desire to join. Neither have the frequent allegations that it is an undemocratic organization, dominated by the major economic powers.

"If the WTO is not democratic, then we will make it democratic," Khandu says confidently. His country is not alone in seeking to join the Geneva-based organization. But unlike the applications of many other prospective members—China, Taiwan, Russia, and Iran, for example—Bhutan's is unlikely to create political controversy.

Bhutan officially describes itself as "the only democratic theocracy in the world." It is the only country in the world which retains the tantric form of Mahayana Buddhism as its official religion. And it is a tiny country, with only 600,000 inhabitants—squeezed between the giant nations of China and India. Bhutan has had good reason to fear for its survival as an independent entity. Its history of seeking security in isolation is understandable. But dipping its toe into global waters has not led to any disastrous consequences so far.

"The experience has been positive: We have no regrets," says Khandra Wangcheck.

* * *

I had interviewed the Bhutanese minister in connection with the UNCTAD meeting in Bangkok, a conference attended by more than 3,000 delegates, mostly diplomats and ministers from developing countries. Only 30 years ago it would have been impossible to persuade such an assembly of the blessings of free trade.

In the 1970s, dependency theory still held sway in most developing countries—and in UNCTAD's corridors in Geneva. According to dependency theory, the developing countries (many of which had just gained independence) could achieve economic development only if they isolated themselves from the old colonial powers. UNCTAD's task was to pave the way for this new economic world order.

A lot has happened since then. As Mark Malloch Brown, head of UNDP, noted in a panel debate: "We are all globalizers now."

Well, perhaps not quite all. Rubens Ricupero, the former Brazilian minister of finance who heads UNCTAD, explained that these days it's the rich countries who fear globalization. Once upon a time, it was the Latin American economists and sociologists who carried the banner for isolation and offered the most systematic critique of "dependency" on the world markets. But nowadays the bulk of anti-globalization literature is produced in the United States and Europe.

The globaphobia which so spectacularly came to the fore at the WTO meeting in Seattle in the winter of 1999, and at the annual meeting of the IMF and the World Bank in Washington, D.C., in April 2000, and in Quebec City in April of 2001, was virtually absent here in Bangkok.

To be sure, the North Korean minister for foreign trade, Kang Jong Mo, gave a speech which was strongly influenced by the teachings of Western globaphobes. And it's easy to be opposed to globalization when the aim of your trade policies is to "glorify the immortal exploits performed by the great leader Comrade Kim Il Sung in the socialist economic construction."

But North Korea's recalcitrance is the exception that proves the rule. Few developing countries today find virtue in isolation. The main message of the conference was that trade must be liberalized further if the poor of the world are to be given a real chance to leave poverty and destitution behind.

"The main losers in today's very unequal world are not those who are too exposed to globalization, but those who have been left out," argued Kofi Annan, secretary general of the United Nations, in his address to the UNCTAD delegates. "Governments [of rich countries] all favor free trade in principle, but too often they lack the political strength to confront those within their own countries who have come to rely on protectionist arrangements."

That was also the main reason why the launch of a new trade round at Seattle had failed, argued Annan.

"The popular myth is that it was blocked" by "a kind of global grass-roots uprising against globalization. The truth, I'm afraid, is more prosaic. The round failed because governments—particularly those of the world's leading economic powers—could not agree on their priorities." Leaders of the developing countries have the responsibility to create a political environment which enables their citizens to prosper from globalization. "Posterity will judge those leaders above all by what they did to encourage the integration of their countries into the global economy, and to ensure that it would benefit all their people."

Posterity will doubtless pass unkind judgments on the leaders of wealthy nations who were unwilling even to discuss trade and development in Bangkok. Sweden was one of the few developed economies represented by the minister for trade. Most sent only ministers carrying the portfolio of foreign aid. The United Sates was represented by a civil servant in the aid administration, the European Union by the commissioner for development aid. Trade, not aid, has long been the message from Western capitals. International trade is superior to international aid as a catalyst for economic development, they have argued. How sad, then, that most developed countries these days seem more comfortable discussing aid than trade with the world's poorest nations. It seems nonsensical to spend billions on debt relief and education and infrastructure in the poorest countries, if the countries are not also given a chance to stand on their own two feet through participation in world markets. `

In this context it was refreshing to hear Clare Short, the secretary for international development in the United Kingdom and a staunch defender of globalization, argue that she wanted to give the world's poorest countries duty free access to the EU market.

Too bad that Short isn't the secretary of trade.

"I have never heard the British secretary for trade take the position that Clare Short did," one EU minister told me.

It is easier to masquerade as a "globalizer" than to actually institute free trade.

* * *

If even as conservative a country as Bhutan can get into the act, does that mean that we are all globalizers now?

Globalization is a process of meshing all the markets of the world into one single, seamless market. And a prerequisite of freedom of trade *between* countries is freedom of trade *within* countries. So one way to assess the headway globalization has been making is to consider how many states are no longer trying to buck the market, no longer trying to pursue a redistributive policy (which can be imposed in a variety of ways, from trade protectionism to transfer systems). Three decades after man set foot on the moon, two decades after Margaret Thatcher inaugurated a new era of market liberalism, one decade after the fall of the Berlin Wall, how far has laissez-faire liberalism been allowed to go? How many of the shackles have been removed?

Let's pick a country as a standard of comparison—say, Sweden. If your country is not at least as free as Sweden, it's not very free.

Sweden is anything but a laissez-faire capitalist society. The state plays a central role in the economy. In the late '90s, the revenue from national taxation equaled 53 percent of GDP—a good deal higher than the already high EU average of 42 percent. Sweden's economic and social life, it is true, is highly internationalized, but the forces of global competition are largely counteracted by domestic policy, not least in the form of traditional distributive policies.

How much of the world's population is living in economies at least more laissez-faire than Sweden's?

The Fraser Institute in Canada has developed an index that measures the degree of economic liberty in 123 countries of the world. Among the factors the index takes into account are national government expenditure, the structure of the economy, the occurrence of price control, monetary policy, exchange control, protection of private ownership, and impediments to trade.

In the 2001 version of the Freedom Index, Sweden ranks 23rd. In other words, as un-free as Sweden is, only 22 countries in the world are considered to be any better off in that respect. Freest of all are Hong Kong, Singapore, New Zealand, the United Kingdom, and the United States. Least free are Burma, Algeria, Congo, Guinea-Bissau, Sierra Leone, and Romania. These 22 relatively free countries have a combined population of around 580 million. In 2001, there were about 6 billion people on this planet; in other words, some 90 percent of the world's population live in societies where the invisible hand of the market is allowed less scope than in Sweden. Of the 580 million who live in countries economically freer than Sweden, only 54 percent live outside the United States of America.

Some say that runaway laissez-faire liberalism is the cause of all the world's poverty, ill health, and injustice. But, considering the data, one wonders if the demonizers are perhaps alluding to a different planet. Where is the neo-liberal and globalist tsunami that the critics deplore? Only 10 percent of the world's population live in countries more economically liberal Sweden. Laissez-faire policy is no more prevalent than that.

We are often told that globalization ruins the nation-state's ability to tax its population. In a world without frontiers, tax bases migrate to tax havens. Thus, social democratic governments can no longer pursue traditional welfare and distributive policy. That is said to be the reality.

The statistics paint another picture. Following an alleged neo-liberal decade (the 1980s) and an alleged decade of globalization (the 1990s), national government expenditure is higher than ever. In 1980 it equaled 25.7 percent of world GDP, according to the World Bank. By 1995 the corresponding figure had risen to 29.1 percent. In the EU, public spending rose from 45.8 percent of GDP in 1980, and to 47.7 percent in 1998. There is nothing in the tables to support the widespread supposition that globalization makes it difficult or impossible for the state to finance its activities through taxation. The left-wing specter of "neo-liberal globalism" is associated rather with an all-time high in taxation and a distributive apparatus of record proportions. Even in the United States, the government is spending more than ever to equalize gaps between high and low income brackets.

Liberty and transparency are not the culprits. It is the walls against trade, the walls that impede the flow of goods and ideas, that preserve poverty and prevent growth. If you want to get rid of the big injustices, if you want to bring better opportunities—for all the inhabitants of the globe—you've got to pull those walls down.

* * *

With Bhutan seeking to become a full-fledged member of the international community, there is hardly a country left that is still trying to cordon itself off completely from the global flows of goods, capital, and information. If Bhutan is on the Web, we are indeed all globalizers now.

But that may be faint praise. Too often, the steps on the road to globalization have been mincing and tentative.

The favor of Lakshmi can be won only by those who take giant strides.

22. Trial by Fire

The roosters crow. A rheumy-eyed old man kicks aside his rake and dashes between the coops to gather the fighters and bring them in from the rain.

"On Sundays we have cockfighting," he tells me. "Come back then."

But betting on poultry wasn't what I had in mind when I came to Navanakorn, an industrial area in the northern outskirts of Bangkok. I'd taken the afternoon off from the UNCTAD conference to find out for myself what globalization looks like up close. The combined chicken farm and gambling den is right next door to a Lucent factory that manufactures microelectronics components— the factory floor of the broadband revolution and the knowledge economy.

The work is done in large square buildings that look like giant sugar cubes. At the entrance stands a shrine honoring Brahma with yellow garlands and small wooden elephants. The white cubes are bedecked with large signs boasting of advanced quality assurance certifications. Inside are thousands of Thai laborers.

"When they started, the workers came on foot. Then they got motorbikes. Now they drive cars," says the rooster guardian. "Everyone wants to work there, but it is hard to get in." Years ago, when the factories were built, no one imagined that the low-salaried workers tramping in from the rice fields would one day be able to afford their very own automobiles. But when Lucent was spun off from AT&T a few years ago, all employees received a hundred stock options, including the assembly line operators of Bangkok. By the end of 1999 and early 2000, when the Bangkok workers were allowed to sell their 100 options, they were worth more than $20,000.

In Thailand, that's a lot of money. No wonder the company's parking lot is crammed with vehicles these days. Cars have replaced bikes; comfortable townhouses have replaced cramped one-room apartments. Children can stay in school for as long as they want, no longer required to leave school to help their families survive.

All thanks to the oft-derided "casino economy" wrought by globalization.

My acquaintance has learned a new term: stock options. He doesn't really understand how they work. But the larger mystery is why someone would give them away—to Thai factory hands! Local companies don't treat their employees this generously. Certainly not the hired hands who rake the leaves and watch over the roosters.

On my way back into town I amble through the industrial estate in search of a ride. A shift is ending. Thousands of women (for it is mostly women who work in the foreign-owned electronics factories) pour through the factory gates. I pass restaurants, drug stores, supermarkets, jewelers, tailors, film shops, vendors of automatic washing machines.

And an elephant.

A family from Surin, a province bordering Cambodia, has set up camp under a green tarpaulin. The elephant is theirs. Her name is Dok Khoon and she is nine years old. "It is too dry at home. There is nothing for her to eat there," explains the boy sitting on the giant beast's back.

The boy and his parents sell bananas for 50 cents; some of the bananas they feed to Dok Khoon. The workers like the elephant. Pregnant women take the opportunity to walk under the creature's belly; that's supposed to bring good luck.

The boy has a warm but shy smile. He is educated and would certainly qualify for work in one of the shining new IT factories.

"But who would then look after the elephant?" he asks me. "We grew up together."

* * *

The battle over globalization is often a battle over "That Which Is Seen, and That Which Is Not Seen."

In his essay of that title, the French economist, politician, and author Frédéric Bastiat (1801–1850) told the story of a child who throws a stone and breaks a window of a good shopkeeper. The shopkeeper must pay six francs to repair the glass. Bad news. But wait, say the onlookers (many of whom are economists). This destructive event is actually a *good* thing. Think of the glazier, who is helped by the fee he receives from you! And the glazier will then pay that six francs to some other person, who will then spend it yet again. Why, the beneficial effects of that stone breaking your window are endless! Rejoice, good sir!

Bastiat distinguished between the bad economist, who concerns himself only with immediate effects, and the good economist, who also takes an interest in long-term effects, i.e., that which cannot be seen but can be foreseen. What is seen when a child throws a stone and breaks a window, is that demand for the glazier's services rises: Industry—a certain industry—is stimulated. What is not seen is that the citizen who must now spend six francs on a new pane of glass is obliged to abstain from spending it on something else, for example a new pair of shoes. Which would have brought income to the shoemaker and stimulated the shoe industry. On net, destruction doesn't pay—except for glaziers.

Those who do battle against global market forces often point to what is seen: for example, the job that is saved when a high tariff stops foreign competition. What they don't see or don't want to acknowledge are the jobs lost—the cost in unnecessary human suffering—as a result of the same high tariff. A tariff designed to stop competition is, on net, an act of destruction that benefits only the immediately protected industry, and then only in the short run. After all, glaziers themselves would not be better off in a world in which stones were constantly being hurled through windows.

Those who hurl bricks through the windows of McDonald's would not be better off in that kind of world, either.

* * *

In some ways, globalization is like writing. When writing first spread throughout the world, it was a very disruptive technology. There were losers and there were winners. Old skills—for example, oral storytelling—became less valuable. A new elite emerged: the elite of the literate. Soon, power was monopolized by those who could exploit reading and writing for their own ends.

Today, every modern activity involves the art of writing in one way or another. Writing has become an unavoidable necessity, a ubiquitous tool that is neither good nor bad in itself. That is not to deny that bad and evil things have been written. But despite all the evil ideas that have been propagated through writing—not least in the century just ended—and despite all the suffering they have caused, no human society could or would want to abolish this invention. It's just not in the cards.

Eventually, globalization will be regarded much the same way. Not as something you want to tamp down or abolish, but as something you want to spread as widely as possible. Like writing, globalization is a powerful tool that can enhance the quality of life. It may yet remain beyond the reach of a large part of humanity—just as writing itself is, even today. India's adult female literacy rate is only 39 percent. Though this populous country boasts a literary tradition that is thousands of years old, 6 out of 10 Indian women cannot read. Cause for indignation? Maybe. But the problem is not that some *can* read and write. The problem is that some *can't*—that not everyone has had the chance to acquire the skill and put it to productive use. "Writing" hasn't failed. India has failed. Same with globalization. The real problem is not that there is too much international buying and selling, but that so many countries have struggled to hamper and curtail it. The failure is one not of markets but of lumbering public policy.

Truly progressive and concerned people will not fight globalization. Instead, they'll fight to overcome the multifarious barriers, at home and abroad, to the spread of globalization.

Thanks to computers, the means of production have become democratized. Today you need neither acres of land nor a factory full of expensive machinery to plunge into international markets. If political barriers were lifted as well, it would be easy for most people to participate in and benefit from global markets.

Each can be the architect of his own future—if he's allowed to be.

But we can't go it alone. We also need viable and nurturing communities, and responsible governments. The protracted stagnation of Europe and the sudden crisis in Asia have taught us that the nation-state still plays a pivotal role in the life of society. Without capable ministers, prescient legislators, just and effective legal systems, globalization will founder. And one or two of these are not enough. We need the whole package.

Going it alone is tempting. Boredom with stuffy politics is understandable. But in practice, exiting the field of politics means surrendering that field to all the old, entrenched lobbies and new power-grabbers—to the trade unions, the agricultural corporations, the pensioners, the moral colonialists, the ski-masked anarchists who throw stones at globalization for the sheer hell of it. If societies are to successfully participate in, and impel, a globalized market economy, a new generation of genuine radical liberals must rise up to make their case, in alliance with entrepreneurs like Mason Su and Seni Williams, and activists like Sumalee and Kim.

Our job is to create a dynamic, open, and tolerant society. A society for masters of the art of living.

* * *

On stage, the noble Phra Ram and his brothers in arms, the monkeys, do battle with Thotsakan, king of the ogres, to free Nang Sida—she who is the reincarnation of Lakshmi, goddess of prosperity.

In the myth of Ramayana, Phra Ram defeats Thotsakan and wins Nang Sida back, after many hard battles. But then he forces her to undergo a trial by fire, to prove that she has been faithful throughout her captivity. She passes this test. But Phra Ram remains suspicious. In the end, he banishes her to the forest.

Disgusted by how she is being treated, Nang Sida descends into the earth.

Will she one day rise again?

Notes

Chapter 1

7 From sluggish backwater to miracle economy. Pasuk Phongpaichit and Chris Baker, *Thailand's Boom and Bust* (Chiang Mai, Thailand: Silkworm Books, 1998).

Chapter 2

10 Growth of Asian foreign investment. *World Investment Report 1998: Trends and Determinants* (New York and Geneva: United Nations Conference on Trade and Development, 1998).

10 Thailand's fast growth. *World Development Report 1997* (New York: Oxford University Press/World Bank, 1997).

11 Globalization as Brazilianization. Hans-Peter Martin and Harald Schumann, *The Global Trap: Globalization and the Assault on Prosperity and Democracy*, trans. Patrick Camiller (New York: Zed Books, 1997).

12 Winner-take-all markets. Thomas L. Friedman, *The Lexus and the Olive Tree* (New York: Farrar, Straus and Giroux, 1999), p. 250.

12 United Coca-Cola. Ulrich Beck, *Vad innebär globaliseringen?* (Göteborg, Sweden: Daidalos, 1998).

13 Brazilianized America. John Gray, "The Brazilianization of the United States," *Fortune* 122, no. 5 (1990).

13 "A mutation in American capitalism." John Gray, *False Dawn: The Delusions of Global Capitalism* (New York: New Press, 1998), pp. 117–18.

13 A new social stratification. Zygmunt Bauman, *Globalization: The Human Consequences* (London: Polity Press, 1998).

14 Alienated symbolic analysts. Robert B. Reich, *The Work of Nations: Preparing Ourselves for 21st Century Capitalism* (New York: Simon & Schuster, 1991).

Chapter 3

15 Police versus mafia. John Lloyd, "Attack on Planet Davos," *Financial Times*, February 24, 2001.

16 Income disparity in Brazil. *World Development Indicators 1998* (Washington: World Bank, 1998).

17 Rocking in Rocinha. Stephen Buckley, "A Slum Sweeps Away Despair," *New York Times*, August 3, 1999.

Chapter 4

19 Nationalism versus liberalism. Marshall C. Eakin, *Brazil: The Once and Future Country* (New York: St. Martin's Griffin, 1998).

19 Low ratio of exports to output. Jeffrey Sachs, "Brazil Fever: First, Do No Harm," *Milken Institute Review* 1, no. 2 (1999), www.milken-inst.org.

21 Pension data. Kenneth Maxwell, "Brazil in Meltdown," *World Policy Journal* 16, no 1 (Spring 1999).

Chapter 5

23 Bangkok's share of industrial output. Chris Dixon, *The Thai Economy: Uneven Development and Internationalisation* (London: Routledge, 1999), p. 192.

25 High Thai tariffs. *World Development Indicators 1998* (Washington: World Bank, 1998).

25 Average incomes by province. "Thailand: Growth, Poverty and Income Distribution," Report No. 15689-TH, World Bank, December 13, 1996.

Chapter 6

30 Amorality of anti-dumping measures. "Anti-Dumping on the WTO Website," www.wto.org/english/tratop_e/adp_e/adp_e.htm.

31 The EC's recent anti-dumping measures. "Eighteenth Annual Report from the Commission to the European Parliament on the Community's Anti-Dumping and Anti-Subsidy Actvities," 1999, europa.eu.int/eurlex/en/com/rpt/2000/com2000_0440en01.pdf.

31 Ring binder mechanisms. "Chinese Ring Binder Fittings," *India-EU News Bulletin* 10, no. 10, October 2000.

31 Mr. Spock rebuffed at the border. Sherrie E. Zhan and Davis P. Goodman, "The Five Issues That Can Make or Break Your Business," *World Trade*, March 1999.

Chapter 7

33 The Seattle protests. David Postman, Jack Broom, and Robert T. Nelson, "Protests, Delay at WTO Warm-up," *Seattle Times*, November 29, 1999.

34 Anti-WTO petition. www.twnside.org.sg/title/wtomr-cn.htm.

35 Clinton on steel import quotas. Philippe Legrain, "Against Globaphobia," *Prospect Magazine*, May 2000.

Chapter 8

39 "Killing America." Patrick J. Buchanan, *The Great Betrayal: How American Sovereignty and Social Justice Are Being Sacrificed to the Gods of the Global Economy* (Boston: Little, Brown and Company, 1998).

39 Gephardt on "fair trade." Dick Gephardt, *An Even Better Place: America in the 21st Century* (New York: Public Affairs, 1999).

40 Promoting fair coffee. Chrystal Cobb, "Students Push Fair Trade Java," *The Davis Enterprise*, December 4, 2000.

40 American protectionist opinion. Albert R. Hunt, "A Short-Term Trade Victory," *Wall Street Journal*, May 25, 2000.

41 Elite opinion of foreign trade. J.E. Reilly, "Americans and the World: A Survey at Century's End," *Foreign Policy* 114 (Spring 1999), pp. 97–114.

43 The logic of protectionism. Steve Chapman, "Our Silly Anti-Dumping Laws," *New Republic*, November 1, 1999.

43 Iranian pistachio nuts. "Nutty," *Forbes*, October 16, 2000.

43 Fruit of the loom versus trade liberalization. "Fruit of the Lobbyist," *Wall Street Journal*, July 24, 1997, p. A18.

Chapter 9

48 Colonialism through trade rules. Jagdish Bhagwati, *A Stream of Windows: Unsettling Reflections on Trade, Immigration, and Democracy* (Cambridge, Mass: MIT Press, 1998).

48 "Social dumping." Keith E. Maskus, "Should Core Labor Standards Be Imposed through International Trade Policy?" Working Paper no. 1817, August 1997 (Washington: World Bank, 1997).

49 Percentage of children working in export industries. "250 Miljoner Barn Arbetar" (Sweden: Save The Children, 2000), www.rb.se/fakta/arbBarn2000/ 250MBarnArb.htm.

50 Efforts to improve working conditions overseas. "Exporting Labor Standards," *Christian Science Monitor*, March 6, 2001.

Chapter 10

53 Trade deficit fallacies. Daniel T. Griswold, "America's Maligned and Misunderstood Trade Deficit," Trade Policy Analysis no. 2, April 20, 1996 (Washington: Cato Institute).

54 Benefits of trade. Dwight R. Lee, "Comparative Advantage," *Ideas on Liberty*, 49, nos. 10 and 11 (1999).

56 Public opinion on protectionism. "Liberalism Lives," *The Economist*, December 31, 1998; "Globalization Blues," *The Economist*, September 28, 2000.

58 U.S. Economic health in 1990s. Francis Fukuyama, *The Great Disruption: Human Nature and the Reconstitution of Social Order* (New York: Free Press, 1999).

59 Ever cheaper. W. Michael Cox and Richard Alm, "Time Well Spent: The Declining *Real* Cost of Living in America," 1997 Annual Report of the Federal Reserve Bank of Dallas, www.dallas-fed.org/htm/pubs/annual/arpt97.html.

Chapter 11

62 The costs of protectionism. "Europe's Burden," *The Economist*, May 22, 1999.

64 Higher duties on poor countries. *Human Development Report 1997* (Oxford: Oxford University Press/United Nations Development Program, 1997).

64 OECD agricultural subsidies. *Trade and Development Report 1999* (New York and Geneva: United Nations Conference on Trade and Development, 1999), p. 136.

65 EU walls. Leif Pagrotsky, Lars Ohly, and Marianne Samuelsson, "EU Måste Visa Mer Solidaritet," *Aftonbladet*, March 10, 1999.

65 Effect of greater employment on European GDP. *World Economic Outlook*, May 1999, International Monetary Fund.

65 Number of antidumping investigations in Europe. European Commission, "Antidumping, Antisubsidy: Statistics Covering the Year 2000," Interim Report 2000/4 (Washington: World Bank, 2001), europa.eu.int/comm/ trade/pdf/adstat2000.pdf.

66 Less than a dollar a day. *World Development Report 2000/2001: Attacking Poverty* (Washington: World Bank, 2001).

Chapter 12

68 Relative wealth of North and South Korea. Samuel S. Kim, *North Korean Foreign Policy in the Post-Cold War Era* (Oxford: Oxford University Press, 1998). Also see *CIA World Factbook 2000*, www.cia.gov/cia/publications/factbook/geos/ks.html and www.cia.gov/cia/publications/factbook/geos/kn.html#Econ/.

69 Capitalist artillery. Karl Marx and Friedrich Engels, *Manifesto of the Communist Party* (Oxford: Oxford World's Classics, 1848, 1998).

Chapter 13

71 Walls in Berlin and Seattle. Moisés Naim, *Foreign Policy*, Spring 2000.

72 The "wall" of either-or thinking. Ulrich Beck, *The Reinvention of Politics: Rethinking Modernity in the Global Social Order* (Cambridge: Polity Press, 1997).

73 ". . .meeting point of all trends and ideologies." Adam Schwartz, *A Nation in Waiting: Indonesia in the 1990s* (St. Leonards, Australia: Allen & Unwin, 1994).

73 Neither-nor. Tony Blair and Gerhard Schröder, *Europe: The Third Way/Die Neue Mitte*, 1999, www.labour.org.uk.

74 Capital must be tamed. Anthony Giddens, *The Third Way: The Renewal of Social Democracy* (Cambridge: Polity Press, 1998).

74 The market did it. *ASEM2 Financial Statement: The Financial and Economic Situation in Asia*, London, April 3, 1998. asem2.fco.gov.uk/asem2/texts/financial.statement.shtml.

Chapter 14

77 Globalization as sunrise. Thomas L. Friedman, *The Lexus and the Olive Tree* (New York: Farrar, Straus and Giroux, 1999), p. xviii.

78 Mercantilism and the base of nations. Deepak Lal, *Unintended Consequences: The Impact of Factor Endowments, Culture, and Politics on Long-Run Economic Performance* (Cambridge, Mass.: MIT Press, 1998).

78 Fukuyama on union politics. Francis Fukuyama, "Second Thoughts: The Last Man in a Bottle," *The National Interest*, no. 56 (Summer 1999).

79 ". . . solidarity, equality, and democratic socialism!" Bertil Jonsson, speech at the Congress of the Social Democratic Party and the Swedish Social Democratic Youth League on August 3, 1999.

79 Be radical. Daniel Singer, *Whose Millennium? Theirs or Ours?* (New York: Monthly Review Press, 1999).

80 The abolition of capitalism. Vänsterpartiet, *För en Solidarisk Värld*. Party platform adopted at the May 31–June 3, 2000, party congress. www. vansterpartiet.se.

80 "Unrestricted" deregulation. Vänsterpartiet. *Internationellt Uttalande*. Adopted at the 1998 party congress. www.vansterpartiet. se/politik/program/intut.html.

80 "Claiming victims every minute." Schlaug, Birger, "Ljus på Kommunismen—Men Vad Händer Bakom Strålkastarna?" *Rörpost*, February 12, 1999. www.mp.se/politik/rorpost/bs_2feb. html.

Chapter 15

83 "Gresham's new law." John Gray, *False Dawn: The Delusions of Global Capitalism* (New York: New Press, 1998).

84 Government expenditure in Burma. *Human Development Report 1999* (New York: Oxford University Press/UNDP, 1999).

85 The french fry's global journey. Richard Read, "The French Fry Connection," *Oregonian*, October 18, 1998. www.oregonlive. com/todaysnews/9810/st101816.html and "The Community of Commerce," *Oregonian*, October 19, 1998. www.oregonlive.com/ todaysnews/9810/st101916.html.

88 In exchange for french fries. David Daniel Kennedy and Lin Yun, *Feng Shui for Dummies* (New York: Hungry Minds, Inc., 2000).

Chapter 16

92 Jiang Zemin on democracy. Matt Pottinger, "China's Jiang Assails Corruption, Shuns Democracy," Reuters, April 1, 2000.

93 ". . . the primordial thing . . ." Ludwig von Mises, *The Anticapitalist Mentality* (Grove City, Pa.: Libertarian Press, 1994), p. 82.

93 Waffling of Asian authoritarians. David Kelly and Anthony Reid (eds.), *Asian Freedoms: The Idea of Freedom in East and Southeast Asia* (Cambridge: Cambridge University Press, 1998).

93 Southern Sung openness and trade. Brian E. McKnight and James T.C. Liu, *The Enlightened Judgments: Ch'ing-ming Chi—The Sung Dynasty Collection* (New York: State University of New York Press, 1999), pp. 21–28.

94 Global Knowledge II. www.globalknowledge.org.my/index_main.htm.

95 Malaysian crackdown. Anil Netto, "Malaysia: Who's Next?" *Asia Times*, April 28, 2001.

96 Hardware without software. *World Development Report 1998/99: Knowledge and Information for Development* (Washington: World Bank, 1999). *Science, Technology and Industry Scoreboard 1999: Benchmarking Knowledge-Based Industries* (Paris: Organization for Economic Co-operation and Development, 1999).

96 Countries with freedom of the press. "Press Freedom Survey 2000" (Washington: Freedom House, 2000). www.freedom house.org/pfs2000/.

97 Reliable information. Jean Michel Severino, "The Power of Information," May 3, 1999. www.worldbank.org/html/extdr/offrep/eap/jmsboard/jmsoped050399.htm.

Chapter 17

99 Trust, norms, and networks. Robert Putnam, *Making Democracy Work: Civic Traditions in Modern Italy* (Princeton, N.J.: Princeton University Press, 1993).

100 Laying foundations "on the ground." Grace Goodell, "The Importance of Political Participation for Sustained Capitalist Development," *Arch. Europ. Sociol.*, XXVI (1985), pp. 93–127.

101 Standards of governance. Rafael La Porta, Florencio Lopez-de-Silanes, Andrei Shleifer, and Robert Vishny, "The Quality of Government," *Journal of Law, Economics, and Organization* 15, no. 1 (1999): 222–79.

Chapter 18

106 Daewoo fraud. John Burton, "34 Daewoo Executives Charged With Accounting Fraud," *Financial Times*, February 19, 2001.

106 The Asian crisis. Stephan Haggard, *The Political Economy of the Asian Financial Crisis* (Washington: Institute for International Economics, 2000). Also see T.J. Pempel (ed.), *The Politics of the Asian Economic Crisis* (Ithaca, N.Y.: Cornell University Press, 1999).

109 Land reform in South Korea. John Lie, *Han Unbound: The Political Economy Of South Korea* (Stanford, Calif.: Stanford University Press, 1998), pp. 11–12.

110 Capitalist on the outside, socialist on the inside. Michael Breen, *The Koreans: Who They Are, What They Want, Where Their Future Lies* (London: Orion Business Books, 1998).

Chapter 19

114 Privileged exceptions. "List Reveals the Privileged KU School Kids," *The Nation*, July 8, 1999.

115 Constitutional ruling against discrimination. "Making Thai History: A Blow to School 'Tea Money' Heralds Positive Change," *Asiaweek*, May 12, 2000.

115 Right of information in India. "Transparency Will Ensure Less Corruption," *The Times of India*, February 16, 2001. www.times ofindia.com/160201/16mpat15.htm.

Chapter 20

119 History and politics of Taiwan. David Shambaugh (ed), *Contemporary Taiwan* (Oxford: Clarendon Press, 1998); Bruce J. Dickson, *Democratization in China and Taiwan: The Adaptability of Leninist Parties* (Oxford: Clarendon Press, 1997); Lee Teng-hui, *The Road to Democracy: Taiwan's Pursuit of Identity* (Tokyo: PHP Institute, 1999).

121 The story of Seni Williams. Karl Maier, *Into the House of the Ancestor: Inside the New Africa* (New York: John Wiley & Sons, 1998).

Chapter 21

130 Index of economic liberty. James Gwartney and Robert Lawson (with Walter Park and James Skipton), *Economic Freedom of the World: Annual Report 2001*, co-published by Fraser Institute, Cato Institute, and others. www.cato.org/ economicfreedom/index.html.

130 Alleged inability to tax the global economy. Gray, *False Dawn*, p. 88. "Tax competition among advanced states works to drain public finances and make a welfare state unaffordable."

130 Government spending higher than ever. *World Development Indicators 1998*.

Chapter 22

134 The glazier's lucky day. Frédéric Bastiat, "That Which Is Seen, and That Which Is Not Seen," in *Selected Essays on Political Economy* (Irvington-on-Hudson, N.Y.: Foundation for Economic Education, 1995).

References

Anti-WTO petition, www.twnside.org.sg/title/wtomr-cn.htm.

1998. *ASEM2 Financial Statement: The Financial and Economic Situation in Asia*, London, April 3. asem2.fco.gov.uk/asem2/texts/financial.statement.shtml.

Asiaweek. 2000. "Making Thai History: A Blow to School 'Tea Money' Heralds Positive Change," May 12.

Bastiat, Frédéric. 1995. "That Which Is Seen, and That Which Is Not Seen" in *Selected Essays on Political Economy*, Irvington-on-Hudson, N.Y.: Foundation for Economic Education.

Bauman, Zygmunt. 1998. *Globalization: The Human Consequences.* London: Polity Press.

Beck, Ulrich. 1997. *The Reinvention of Politics: Rethinking Modernity in the Global Social Order.* Cambridge: Polity Press.

———. 1998. *Vad Innebär Globaliseringen?* Göteborg, Sweden: Daidalos.

Bhagwati, Jagdish. 1998. *A Stream of Windows: Unsettling Reflections on Trade, Immigration, and Democracy.* Cambridge, Mass.: MIT Press.

Blair, Tony, and Gerhard Schröder. 1999. *Europe: The Third Way/Die Neue Mitte.* www.labour.org.uk.

Breen, Michael. 1998. *The Koreans: Who They Are, What They Want, Where Their Future Lies.* London: Orion Business Books.

Buchanan, Patrick J. 1998. *The Great Betrayal: How American Sovereignty And Social Justice Are Being Sacrificed to the Gods of the Global Economy.* Boston: Little, Brown and Company.

Buckley, Stephen. 1999. A Slum Sweeps Away Despair. *New York Times* (August 3).

Burton, John. 2001. 34 Daewoo Executives Charged with Accounting Fraud. *Financial Times* (February 19).

Chapman, Steve. 1999. Our Silly Anti-Dumping Laws. *New Republic* (November 1).

Christian Science Monitor. 2001. Exporting Labor Standards (March 6).

CIA World Factbook 2000. www.cia.gov/cia/publications/factbook/geos/ks.html and http://www.cia.gov/cia/publications/factbook/geos/kn.html#Econ/.

Cobb, Chrystal. 2000. Students Push Fair Trade Java. *The Davis Enterprise* (December 4).

Cox, W. Michael and Richard Alm. 1997. Time Well Spent: The Declining *Real* Cost of Living in America. 1997 Annual Report of the Federal Reserve Bank of Dallas. www.dallasfed.org/htm/pubs/annual/arpt97.html.

Dickson, Bruce J. 1997. *Democratization in China and Taiwan: The Adaptability of Leninist Parties.* Oxford: Clarendon Press.

Dixon, Chris. 1999. *The Thai Economy: Uneven Development and Internationalisation.* London: Routledge, 192.

Eakin, Marshall C. 1998. *Brazil: The Once and Future Country.* New York: St. Martin's Griffin.

Economist. 1998. Liberalism Lives (December 31).

——. 1999. Europe's Burden (May 22).

——. 2000. Globalization Blues (September 28).

European Commission. 1999. Eighteenth Annual Report from the Commission to the European Parliament on the Community's Anti-Dumping and Anti-Subsidy Actvities. europa.eu.int/eur-lex/en/com/rpt/2000/com2000_0440en01.pdf.

——. 2001. Antidumping, Antisubsidy: Statistics Covering the Year 2000, Interim Report 2000/4. Washington: World Bank. europa.eu.int/comm/trade/pdf/adstat2000.pdf.

Forbes. 2000. "Nutty," October 16.

Freedom House. 2000. Press Freedom Survey 2000. www.freedom house.org/pfs2000/.

Friedman, Thomas L. 1999. *The Lexus and the Olive Tree.* New York: Farrar, Straus and Giroux.

Fukuyama, Francis. 1999a. *The Great Disruption: Human Nature and the Reconstitution of Social Order.* New York: Free Press.

———. 1999b. Second Thoughts: The Last Man in a Bottle. *The National Interest*, no. 56 (Summer).

Gephardt, Dick. 1999. *An Even Better Place: America in the 21st Century.* New York: Public Affairs.

Giddens, Anthony. 1998. *The Third Way: The Renewal of Social Democracy.* Cambridge: Polity Press.

Goodell, Grace. 1985. The Importance of Political Participation for Sustained Capitalist Development. Archives Europeenes De Sociologie. XXVI, pp. 93–127.

Gray, John. 1990. The Brazilianization of the United States. *Fortune* 122, no. 5.

———. 1998. *False Dawn: The Delusions of Global Capitalism.* New York: New Press, 117–18.

Griswold, Daniel T. 1996. America's Maligned and Misunderstood Trade Deficit. Trade Policy Analysis no. 2 (April 20). Washington: Cato Institute.

Gwartney, James, and Robert Lawson (with Walter Park and James Skipton). 2001. *Economic Freedom of the World: Annual Report 2001,* co-published by Fraser Institute, Cato Institute, and others, www.cato.org/economicfreedom/index.html.

Haggard, Stephan. 2000. *The Political Economy of the Asian Financial Crisis.* Washington: Institute for International Economics. Also see T.J. Pempel (ed.). 1999. *The Politics of the Asian Economic Crisis.* Ithaca, N.Y.: Cornell University Press.

Hunt, Albert R. 2000. A Short-Term Trade Victory. *Wall Street Journal* (May 25); Chinese Ring Binder Fittings. *India-EU News Bulletin* 10, no. 10 (October).

International Monetary Fund. 1999. *World Economic Outlook*, May.

Jonsson, Bertil. 1999. Speech at the Congress of the Social Democratic Party and the Swedish Social Democratic Youth League on August 3.

Kelly, David, and Anthony Reid (eds.). 1998. *Asian Freedoms: The Idea of Freedom in East and Southeast Asia.* Cambridge: Cambridge University Press.

Kennedy, David Daniel, and Lin Yun. 2000. *Feng Shui for Dummies.* New York: Hungry Minds, Inc.

Kim, Samuel S. 1998. *North Korean Foreign Policy in the Post-Cold War Era.* Oxford: Oxford University Press.

Krueger, Anne O., and Junghoo Yoo. 2001. *Chaebol* Capitalism and the Currency Financial Crisis in Korea. *NBER* Conference Paper.

La Porta, Rafael, Florencio Lopez-de-Silanes, Andrei Shleifer, and Robert Vishny. 1999. The Quality of Government. *Journal of Law, Economics, and Organization* 15, no. 1: 222–79.

Lal, Deepak. 1998. *Unintended Consequences: The Impact of Factor Endowments, Culture, and Politics on Long-Run Economic Performance.* Cambridge, Mass.: MIT Press.

Lee, Dwight R. 1999. Comparative Advantage. *Ideas on Liberty* 49, nos. 10 and 11.

Legrain, Philippe. 2000. Against Globaphobia. *Prospect Magazine* (May).

Lie, John. 1998. *Han Unbound: The Political Economy Of South Korea.* Stanford, Calif.: Stanford University Press, pp. 11–12.

Lloyd, John. 2001. Attack on Planet Davos. *Financial Times* (February 24).

Maier, Karl. 1998. *Into the House of the Ancestor: Inside the New Africa.* New York: John Wiley & Sons.

Martin, Hans-Peter, and Harald Schumann. 1997. *The Global Trap: Globalization and the Assault on Prosperity and Democracy,* trans. Patrick Camiller. New York: Zed Books.

Marx, Karl, and Friedrich Engels. 1848. *Manifesto of the Communist Party.* Oxford: Oxford World's Classics, 1998.

Maskus, Keith E. 1997. Should Core Labor Standards Be Imposed through International Trade Policy? Working Paper no. 1817, August. Washington: World Bank.

Maxwell, Kenneth. 1999. Brazil in Meltdown. *World Policy Journal* 16, no. 1 (Spring).

McKnight, Brian E., and James T.C. Liu. 1999. *The Enlightened Judgments: Ch'ing-ming Chi—The Sung Dynasty Collection.* New York: State University of New York Press, pp. 21–8.

Mises, Ludwig von. 1994. *The Anticapitalist Mentality*. Grove City, Pa.: Libertarian Press, p. 82.

Naim, Moisés. 2000. *Foreign Policy* (Spring).

Nation, The. 1999. List Reveals the Privileged KU School Kids (July 8).

Netto, Anil. 2001. Malaysia: Who's Next? *Asia Times* (April 28).

Organization for Economic Cooperation and Development. 1999. *Science, Technology and Industry Scoreboard 1999: Benchmarking Knowledge-Based Industries*. Paris.

Pagrotsky, Leif, Lars Ohly, and Marianne Samuelsson. 1999. EU Måste Visa Mer Solidaritet. *Aftonbladet* (March 10).

Phongpaichit, Pasuk, and Chris Baker. 1998. *Thailand's Boom and Bust*. Chiang Mai, Thailand: Silkworm Books.

Postman, David, Jack Broom, and Robert T. Nelson. 1999. Protests, Delay at WTO Warm-up. *Seattle Times* (November 29).

Pottinger, Matt. 2000. China's Jiang Assails Corruption, Shuns Democracy. Reuters (April 1).

Putnam, Robert. 1993. *Making Democracy Work: Civic Traditions in Modern Italy*. Princeton, N.J.: Princeton University Press.

Read, Richard. 1998a. The French Fry Connection. *Oregonian* (October 18).

———. 1998b. The Community of Commerce. *Oregonian* (October 19.)

Reich, Robert B. 1991. *The Work of Nations: Preparing Ourselves for 21st Century Capitalism*. New York: Simon & Schuster.

Reilly, J.E. 1999. Americans and the World: A Survey at Century's End. *Foreign Policy* 114 (Spring): 97–114.

Sachs, Jeffrey. 1999. Brazil Fever: First, Do No Harm. *Milken Institute Review* 1, no. 2. www.milken-inst.org.

Save the Children. 2000. 250 Miljoner Barn Arbetar. www.rb.se/fakta/arbBarn2000/250MBarnArb.htm.

Schlaug, Birger. 1999. Ljus på Kommunismen—Men Vad Händer Bakom Strålkastarna? *Rörpost* (February 12). www.mp.se/politik/rorpost/bs_2feb.html.

Schwartz, Adam. 1994. *A Nation in Waiting: Indonesia in the 1990s* (St. Leonards, Australia: Allen & Unwin.

Severino, Jean Michel. 1999. The Power of Information. May 3. www.worldbank.org/html/extdr/offrep/eap/jmsboard/jmsoped 050399.htm.

Shambaugh, David (ed.). 1998. *Contemporary Taiwan.* Oxford: Clarendon Press.

Singer, Daniel. 1999. *Whose Millennium? Theirs or Ours?* New York: Monthly Review Press.

Teng-hui, Lee. 1999. *The Road to Democracy: Taiwan's Pursuit of Identity.* Tokyo: PHP Institute.

Times of India. 2001. Transparency Will Ensure Less Corruption. (February 16). www.timesofindia.com/160201/16mpat15.htm.

United Nations Conference on Trade and Development. 1998. *World Investment Report 1998: Trends and Determinants.* New York and Geneva.

———. 1999. *Trade and Development Report 1999.* New York and Geneva.

United Nations Development Program. 1997. *Human Development Report 1997.* Oxford: Oxford University Press.

Vänsterpartiet. 1998. *Internationellt uttalande.* Adopted at the 1998 party congress, www.vansterpartiet.se/politik/program/intut. html.

———. 2000. *För en Solidarisk Värld.* Party platform adopted at the May 31–June 3 party congress, www.vansterpartiet.se.

Wall Street Journal. 1997. Fruit of the Lobbyist (July 24): A18.

World Bank. 1996. *Thailand: Growth, Poverty and Income Distribution,* Report No. 15689-TH, December 13.

———. 1997. *World Development Report 1997.* New York: Oxford University Press.

———. 1998. *World Development Indicators 1998.* Washington: World Bank Report.

———. 1999. *World Development Report 1998/99: Knowledge and Information for Development.* Washington: World Bank Report.

———. 2001. *World Development Report 2000/2001: Attacking Poverty.*

World Trade Organization, Anti-Dumping on the WTO Website. www.wto.org/english/tratop_e/adp_e/adp_e.htm.

Zhan, Sherrie E., and Davis P. Goodman. 1999. The Five Issues That Can Make or Break Your Business. *World Trade* (March).

Index

157

About the Author

Tomas Larsson is a Swedish journalist who spent 10 years reporting from Thailand. He was a correspondent for *Business Asia*, a Hong Kong-based newsletter published by the Economist Intelligence Unit, and he has written for the Swedish dailies *Svenska Dagbladet* and *Finanstidningen,* as well as *Vagabond,* the *Financial Times,* and the *Far Eastern Economic Review.* He is the author of several books published by Timbro, a public policy institute in Stockholm, including *Asiens kris är inte kapitalismens.* He now lives with his Thai-born wife, Chanita, and their two daughters in Ithaca, New York, where he is studying for a Ph.D. in government at Cornell University.

A World Connected

aWorldConnected.org, a project of the Institute for Humane Studies at George Mason University, fosters an understanding of how globalization improves the lives of people around the world.

For more information on the topic of globalization—debates, links to key websites, and other intellectual resources—visit www.aWorldConnected.org.

Founded in 1961, the Institute for Humane Studies is a non-profit educational institute that offers scholarships, seminars, internships, and other student-oriented programs. IHS seeks to advance an understanding of how people can live cooperatively in a world that is peaceful, prosperous, and free.

Cato Institute

Founded in 1977, the Cato Institute is a public policy research foundation dedicated to broadening the parameters of policy debate to allow consideration of more options that are consistent with the traditional American principles of limited government, individual liberty, and peace. To that end, the Institute strives to achieve greater involvement of the intelligent, concerned lay public in questions of policy and the proper role of government.

The Institute is named for *Cato's Letters*, libertarian pamphlets that were widely read in the American Colonies in the early 18th century and played a major role in laying the philosophical foundation for the American Revolution.

Despite the achievement of the nation's Founders, today virtually no aspect of life is free from government encroachment. A pervasive intolerance for individual rights is shown by government's arbitrary intrusions into private economic transactions and its disregard for civil liberties.

To counter that trend, the Cato Institute undertakes an extensive publications program that addresses the complete spectrum of policy issues. Books, monographs, and shorter studies are commissioned to examine the federal budget, Social Security, regulation, military spending, international trade, and myriad other issues. Major policy conferences are held throughout the year, from which papers are published thrice yearly in the *Cato Journal*. The Institute also publishes the quarterly magazine *Regulation*.

In order to maintain its independence, the Cato Institute accepts no government funding. Contributions are received from foundations, corporations, and individuals, and other revenue is generated from the sale of publications. The Institute is a nonprofit, tax-exempt, educational foundation under Section 501(c)3 of the Internal Revenue Code.

CATO INSTITUTE
1000 Massachusetts Ave., N.W.
Washington, D.C. 20001